DAKOTA WARRIOR

The Story of J. R. Weddell

Gloria Mattioni
with Daniele Bolelli

With a new update and a new afterword by the author, plus an additional chapter on the history of the struggle for the Black Hills by Daniele Bolelli.

Copyright © 2014 Gloria Mattioni
All rights reserved.
ISBN-10: 1495963853
ISBN-13: 978-1495963858

*In Spirit and friendship,
Mitakuye Oyasin!*

For Cicily Weddell

Cicily and her dad, James R. Weddell

Acknowledgments

I owe many thanks to the large numbers of people who have contributed to this project. First and foremost, to the Weddell *tiyospaye* that I consider my own Ihanktonwan family, for their trust, friendship, and support, and particularly to Sam, the big brother and chief whom everybody would want to have, and Mercy, the sister whom I relied on most for help when nobody knew me yet. I owe

Daniele Bolelli and Hazel Weddell, James' mother

special thanks to Hazel Weddell, James' mom and first supporter, who welcomed me into the family without hesitation, treating me like her "tenth daughter", sharing with me endless stories and secrets that helped to keep me safe in times of danger. I know she's smiling from wherever she's at now, seeing her beloved Jimmy's face on the cover of this book.

I have a debt of gratitude also with my son, Daniele Bolelli, who not only contributed to this book a chapter about the Black Hills struggle, but also accompanied me in great summer adventures throughout Indian country, visiting James in different prisons and being a great friend and supporter to him since day One, spending plenty of sleepless nights helping me to sort documents and elaborate strategies to get Jim out.

I also want to acknowledge Evelyn Tiger, her sisters and Grandma Lois Tiger for their continuous support to James, for whom they always kept a spot in their hearts; Cyndi Weddell, James' wife, whom he married in 2005; Bruce Allen, who has been a close friend to Jim in his last years spent in Flandreau, on the Santee reservation, and who has been enthusiastic about the project of this book providing a good number of initial orders; my husband, Federico Giordano, who volunteered his graphic skills to the layout and had the patience to retouch very old pictures with photoshop making them printable; and of course all the people who ordered this book before it even went to print. Without you all, I wouldn't have made it.

DAKOTA WARRIOR

The Story of
JAMES R. WEDDELL

James and Gloria the day he walked free, December 18th, 2003

Prologue

This book tells the story of James R. Weddell, a Yankton-Sioux native who spent big part of his life behind bars because of racism and injustice.

The book was first published in Italy by Sensibili Alle Foglie, in 1995. It was then reprinted by another publisher, Edizioni l'Età dell'Acquario in 1998, and used to raise funds for the legal proceedings to pursue James R. Weddell's freedom in court. It was also self-published by supporters in

France but never in the U.S. since some of the stories told could have prejudiced James' battle to regain his freedom.

Gloria Mattioni is a published author, journalist and documentary producer. She met James in 1993 and immediately embraced his cause, starting an investigation to reopen the case and spending the following ten years at James' side, until victory in court was achieved. She also wrote, directed and produced a documentary, *Give Me Back My Land, Give Me Back My Freedom*, together with Osvaldo Verri and Stefano Scotti. The documentary was screened at festivals and social centers in Italy to publicize James' story. The book and documentary generated a large increase in solidarity and support for James' cause.

James R. Weddell finally walked free on December 18th, 2003

Brother Sam Weddell, James, Cicily, granddaughter Aiyana and friend Joe Lovell in 2003.

In 1986, he had been charged with a crime he didn't commit, and sent to prison with an eighty-year sentence. He spent sixteen years in prison and two years on the run, after his escape from South Dakota State Penitentiary in 1987. While on the run, James was hidden by friends, relatives and supporters all over the American Indian reservations of South Dakota. He was eventually caught in May 1989, after being featured on the TV show America's Most Wanted and thanks to a bounty on his head. Another fifteen years for escaping were added to his existing sentence.

Even in the darkest hours, when he had to stand alone, his spirit was never broken. He kept fighting, sustained by his beliefs, convinced that his victory could "show the whole Indian nation that it's worth fighting the system on its own ground, and it can be done." He also continued to pursue the return of the *Paha Sapa*, or Black Hills, the Lakota sacred lands that were illegally acquired by the U.S. government.

Once out of prison, James took back his place as a defender of his people's rights.
His probation terms did not allow him to live on the Yankton Sioux Reservation, so he first moved to Rapid City, and later to Flandreau, on the Santee reservation.
He was, and still is, a role model for young warriors, and is deeply missed by his family and friends. He died in a car accident on October 26, 2013, on a rural road seventeen miles out of Wagner, SD, where he was born and raised.
This new edition of the book covers the last 10 years of his life as well as the four-day wake and service held at the National Guard Armory, in Wagner. Hundreds came to say their last goodbyes to James, who was honored like a chief of old times. Another chapter about the Black Hills dispute, written by Daniele Bolelli, American History and Native American Studies professor at Cal-State University of Long Beach, has also been added

Night Call

October 26th, 2013, had been a rough day. I felt like I was catching something. I kept pushing and working despite my headache and chest congestion. It was Friday, after all. The weekend around the corner gave me hope. I missed a good night sleep. I hadn't had one in a while. I turned off my phone before going to bed. Having family, friends, and business across the ocean makes my phone ring at the craziest hours. People in Italy tend to forget that I live in a different time zone, or call me thinking that there is a six-hour difference between Italy and Los Angeles, just like there is between Italy and New York. On top of that, I learned to fear the ring of a night call since the time my sister was in hospital for a long while, suspended on the edge between life and death. I still have nightmares about those phone rings piercing the darkness of the night. So my phone stayed off, until 7 a.m.

When I turned the phone on, there were two messages on my voicemail, left around 2 a.m. The first was from Cicily, James' daughter, and the second from his sister Mercy. I got chills down my spine only looking at their names and the odd time of their calls. James had not been feeling good in a while. His heart had been acting up. Medical tests showed that three of the four valves were leaking and he kept having episodes characterized by doctors as mini-strokes. Last time we met, a couple of months earlier, at the end of summer by the Lode Star Casino in Fort Thompson, he was just out of the hospital. They had inserted a catheter from an artery in his arm to his heart, to check on its malfunctioning. The results didn't seem to worry doctors enough, but James surely didn't look good. He had stopped working, and was feeling insecure about his health.

This feeling was not based on facts and hospital charts. No matter what the medical reports said, James was convinced that he was going to die soon. "I'm going around to say all my goodbyes", he had told me on the phone. "Spirits came to tell me I'll be gone before Christmas. I'm ready. In many ways, I want to go."

He had not been his cheerful self for a while now. Our last call happened just a couple of days earlier, and he sounded depressed. "I feel weak", he had said, and it had seemed so unreal to me. Him weak? The strongest man I ever met? The warrior who never feared tostand alone, whose spirit couldn't be broken? "I am broken", he had insisted. "I'm dying but that isn't the worst part. I feel lonely. I don't fit. I see everybody on my reservation and others too, going around in big cars, turning on 50" flat screen televisions as soon as they enter their doors, their kids having their personal Ipad and Iphone or Xbox, spoiled rotten with so many material things while some elders don't even have enough propane to keep them warm… It isn't as I wish it was, as it was once when people really cared about each other, were really friends."

I had tried to soothe his mood, make him realize how many people really loved him and cared for him, how many friends he had around. But he wasn't convinced. He was the embodiment of a chief of old times. He should have lived then, when everybody would put the people first. "First comes the tribe, everybody's good, and only then the individual. That's how it was and it should be. That's how I will always feel."

Jim was somebody who walked his talk. His words were not wind. He would help anybody, and sometimes people abused his generosity. In the last months, despite his illness, he kept getting calls from left and right, from people whose relatives were dying. They didn't feel strong enough to be standing by their loved ones in their final hours so they called on James for support. He'd always go. "Anytime this phone rings, somebody is dying and they need my help. I go, but it's taking a toll on me… all this death business."

I had begged him not to go, to care about himself too, say no when he wasn't in good enough shape for it, but Jim had said: "I have to. It's my duty as a warrior. If I don't, they have nobody else. There is nobody else left to answer the call for something like this."

I had talked with Cicily and we were planning a big surprise party, a celebration for the upcoming anniversary of his ten years of freedom. Something to cheer him up, make him feel the kinship of his big clan, the Weddell *tiyospaye*. Something to warm up his beaten heart with lots of laughter, good food and music, storytelling, maybe even a "new" used truck for him: a collective present so he wouldn't have to borrow others' cars to get around, once winter arrived.

I had dropped a couple of hints about it in our conversation, and Jim had said: "I still can't handle crowds too good. Remember that. I didn't even go to the Weddell reunion last summer, didn't feel comfortable. I'd rather celebrate with only a few at a time." But Cis and I didn't want to believe him. "He'll come around", we kept repeating to ourselves, "and when he sees how many came for him, it will make him feel better."

I had not wanted to listen to him either when he said he was going to die soon, and tried to give instructions for his funeral. "Come on! Christmas will come, and you'll be decorating trees for the kids and opening presents."

But it wasn't Christmas yet. It was October 27th, and there were those two messages on my voicemail, left at 2 a.m.

James had passed. He was in a car accident on the

Sister Mercy with James

road to Greenwood and the cemetery, down by the river. That's what Mercy's message said.
Cicily had only asked me to call as soon as I got her call, but Mercy had said it like it was.

It didn't seem possible. It felt unreal. "I want to be ninety and all gray, with a   bunch of grandchildren sitting in my lap", he had said. And I always thought that was the plan. That's what would have been written on his stone. I was shaking but I gathered all my strength and called back.

"When it happens, you don't cry. I don't want you to cry. I want you there." I had promised that I would go just to make him stop talking about his imminent death—something that I refused to consider a real possibility. I would have gone no matter what. I don't like funerals. I attended only a couple in my whole life. I never even went to my father's. But James'? No way I would have missed it. I wanted to see him one last time, and be there to help the family send him on to the other side in the best possible way. That's what he wanted. He had made sure to tell Cicily how to do it all, pinning her down to write his instructions despite her protests. That's what he would get. I booked the first flight to

A wolf hide to protect James' journey

Sioux Falls I could get on, not knowing exactly what to expect, not caring about anything else but being there. I arrived in Wagner in the evening around 7 pm, and went straight to the Armory downtown. I had not driven along those country roads in a long time but they were still so vivid in my memory. I thought next time I'd be on

Xander in full regalia, dancing at a PowWow

those roads, Jim wouldn't, and felt a knot in my throat. "Don't cry", he had said. So I didn't. But lots of others were, when I entered the hall where Jim had been laid to rest.

There was a spread of colorful star blankets hung on the wall behind the sacred bundle, an open coffin that would be later wrapped in the buffalo hide it was laying on. There were foldable tables for the whole length of the wall behind the bundle filled with family photos, memories and objects that various people had brought to honor James R. Weddell. A wolf hide to protect his journey. A traditional drum, different from what was going to be played by the singers. Jim's fan of eagle feathers, that was going to be passed down to Xander, his *takoja,* the grandson born only a few days after Jim's release from prison, who had become, to his pride, a traditional singer and dancer like Jim's younger brother, Mike. Xander would also be inheriting something else: Jim's claim to the Black Hills; that "bloody money" that he had refused at the highest cost—his most precious legacy. This was a story that Xander, and the rest of us, would keep telling for the days to come, for the new generations of Dakota warriors.

Before leaving Los Angeles in a hurry, I had only managed to grab a copy of the book, "Dakota Warrior", which was published in Italy in 1995, but never in the U.S. Jim and I had recently talked about publishing a new book here in America. I thought the project might have made him feel better, and Jim had said: "We can add on new chapters and updates, but the core of the new book must be the old one. Because it was darn good! And none of my family read it since it was written in Italian. I want them to know how I was feeling all those years when I was gone." So I put the book there on the table, together with the rest of the honors, and people started to come over where I was standing, asking me about it. They didn't know much about it, but they said they'd love to read it.

My attention to their words in that moment was limited, though. I just wanted to see Jim, maybe still secretly hoping he wasn't there, that I'd go by the coffin, lift the veil, and there would be a puppet laying there in his place, and the whole thing turned out to be just one of his badass jokes.

Instead, there he was. Still looking good, but so cold. I kissed his cheek and his skin felt icy. His mouth was closed, his hands folded on his stomach. He looked peaceful, like he was just taking a nap. "I don't want you to cry." But lots of others were.

The sacred bundle, where James rests wrapped in a buffalo hide.

He was already missed by so many. The adults were the ones crying. The kids would go by the coffin, lift the veil and touched him like it was a game, like their great *deksi*, uncle, or grandpa was ready to jump out and scare them all, laughing. It was good to see the children act normally, not being affected. There is always a bunch of children at Indian ceremonies, which make them feel more real, more like a part of everyday life. Many of these children were just babies when I was here the last time. They would go by their grandma, pulling her skirt and asking: "that lady busted him out of prison?"—as if we had been Bonnie and Clyde, and I could almost hear Jim laughing out loud, "those kids!"

They told me it was a bad accident. It was late, past midnight when he left Cicily's house in the car he had borrowed from Sam. Jim wasn't wearing his belt. How ironic for somebody who'd always tell others "drive safe and buckle up." He was a great driver. The only possible explanation: either he had fallen asleep at the wheel or a deer had jumped out of a ditch all of a sudden. In fact, there were skid marks showing that the car had crossed toward the other side of the road all of a sudden, ending down the slope in the opposite ditch. James was projected out the window and kept rolling 30 feet. His neck was broken and, the doctor said, he died on the spot.

Later, I asked Jason to bring me by the place. I still had troubles accepting that it really happened, that this wasn't but a bad dream. It was hard to go by the place and see the shattered glass from the car windows, the spot where the weeds were all bent there in the ditch. I tried to halt my mind and keep it still, forbidding it to play the film of the accident as it was starting to roll. "Perhaps when my day come I will be alone", Jim had texted me in a message about a month before, when a great elder, the *akicita* Pat Big Eagle, had passed. "Maybe in some meadow. Maybe by the river." Let's go back to the others.

Drumming at the wake

Let's hang tight, all together.
I slept at Julie's house, where I had stayed with Jim in 2003, the first nights after he was released. Memories were overwhelming and I couldn't get asleep. "I don't want you to cry" resonated in my ears, and I knew Jim could see me even when nobody else could. And yet, I was so grateful to Julie for letting me crash with her since I couldn't take being alone in a motel room.

    I also wanted to go say hello to Sam, who was at his house where the fire was kept going in the teepee, all day and night. It was going to burn for four days, according to tradition, thanks to little Larry, Eric and other nephews, determined to honor their *deksi* in the best way. They did such a good job—those young warriors. His nieces, meanwhile, were doing the most amazing job in the kitchen to feed everybody. No matter how many come, you got to feed the people. That's how it was, is and should be. And the food at Jim's wake, with hundreds coming from all South Dakota reservations and other states too, was incredibly good. I wasn't hungry but I had learned long ago to honor a feast that has been put up with so much love and dedication. No matter if I was an almost-vegetarian, I ate the buffalo soup that was served at the end of the day. And I wolfed down the fry bread and the chokeberry pudding, recalling how fond Jim was of them.

As delicious as the food was, the storytelling was still the best part. People from all walks took the microphone to share their stories of Jim. And they were all great stories. Those who had hidden him in their houses when he was a fugitive on the run weren't afraid of coming out in the open now. Their stories were the most intriguing, making the audience crack up in loud laughter here and there. Indian humor. Something I've always appreciated because it keeps you going—laughing in the face of despair.

It felt good to see Jim honored for the chief he'd always been. "In ancient times, he would have been chief of this tribe. He should have been", I had said when it was my turn at the microphone. It felt good to see even his "enemies" there, those who had betrayed him, coming by to pay their last respects. And it felt good to meet the whole family again. I had missed them a lot and I was in awe for the incredible effort they had put up in such a short time, despite their grief.

Aiyana, "Yani", Cicily's daughter, was no longer the little girl I had left seven years earlier. She had grown into a stunning young woman. So had Bella, Jodi's only girl who had spent the night with Yani in the Armory to keep company to Jim, now bouncing on her shoulders Hendrix Z., her little nephew, the first great grandson of Sam and Petite. I

realized how much I had missed out in these last years of separation, and thought how much Jim had missed out during all the years he was kept away from his family. "We were just starting to make up for it", Cicily said, holding back her tears. "We still had lots of bonding to do." The bond, though, had always been there. No matter how many miles, prison walls or even death, Jim loved his family with all his heart, and they loved him back.
He will never be forgotten. This world will never be the same without him but he will live forever in the hearts of his family and friends.

"Keep your hearts pure then", said David Arrow, a

Niece Jody Zephier with James

traditional spiritual leader whom Jim had chosen to officiate his service. Jim's heart was. He had the heart and the smile of a child. He was as spiritual as he was brave.

And as much as I know that I will miss my friend in a terrible way, I am relieved that he had known in advance that his day was coming, and had time to prepare.

He went home, like we all kept repeating at his wake.

He went on to be reunited with his mom and dad, sisters and brother who had already gone to the spirit world, chiefs of his and other times, and all the Dakota warriors who had walked in the same path before him.

Hoka-hey, Jim, ahò ahò ahò. You chose a good day, a good way to die.

Xander and David Arrow guide the pallbearers taking James away

DAKOTA WARRIOR

What follows is the original book that Gloria Mattioni wrote and published in Europe in 1995, and 1998—a two voice narrative based on hundreds of letters, phone conversations and visits that she had with James in 1993 and 1994, the first two years of their twenty-year long friendship

CONTENTS

Introduction	(Gloria)
A Dakota Warrior	(James)
Encounter in Prison	(Gloria)
The Earth Keepers	(James)
White Justice	(Gloria)
On the Run	(James)
Dreams and Visions	(Gloria)
International Solidarity	(James)

Introduction

I met James for the first time in a dream. It happened long before I knew of his existence. Months before anyone had spoken to me about him.

It was 1992, and I had recently moved to Los Angeles, California, in between the L.A. riots and a 5.6 quake—both events that rocked heavily the "city of dreams". I never felt at home in my native Italy. I was a born traveler and had chosen a job that allowed me to pursue my adventures around the world. I was also a storyteller, and writing about people's lives was my call. Over the previous four years, I had extensively traveled the U.S., spending time on different Native American reservations and getting acquainted with a way of life that I had always respected. In 1992, I was writing my first book, and had scaled down my activities as a journalist, tired of typical magazine article approach to storytelling that rarely goes beyond a superficial level. Moving to Los Angeles gave me the necessary distance from my previous life. Changing the scenery around me seemed to go hand in hand with my desire for a change of direction. I had no clear ideas about the future. I didn't know what I wanted to or should do with my life.

"Writing is a cry against corruption," I had read in a book by Katherine Mansfield, and until then it had seemed to be enough. But then I began to ask myself, "Is it enough to cry out in a world with so much evil and corruption?" I felt in my bones that action should accompany words. I had been a political activist when living in Italy. But the path of political struggle that I had practiced in the past hadn't lead to the results I craved. I didn't feel like I had been able to make a difference the way I wanted to.

In my dream, I saw this man sitting on the floor of a cell. He was both sick and lonely. I saw his face clearly. It was obvious he was a Native American but I was unable to figure out what tribe he came from. His nose was thin and sharp; his eyes had a deep gaze despite the suffering. He had long hair, which was held on his forehead by a red bandana. He was strong and muscular, but didn't seem tall. When I woke up, the images were still very vivid. I thought I heard a name in the dream, but I wasn't sure about this. The only things I was certain of were that I had to help the man sitting in that cell, and that the dream had come to call me to act. He was sick—very sick. He was unable to support his head, and wore a neck-brace around his neck like those worn by people after they've been in an accident.

I had this dream in October 1992, when James was held in a federal facility in Marion, Illinois. He was indeed in prison at that time, but still in full health. A couple of months later, however, on December 30, during the transfer that finally took him back to his native land in South Dakota, the van transporting him was involved in a bad wreck. James was bounced from one side to the other of the van—thrown around like clothes in a dryer. Contrary to legal requirements, the cage in which he was held along with another prisoner had seats but no seatbelts. James suffered injuries to his arms and legs together with a concussion that left him unconscious for several hours. While the white prisoner was immediately offered medical treatment, including a CT scan and magnetic resonance, James was simply given twenty-seven (27!) Tylenol to numb the pain.

From that day onward, his suffering worsened. He was in dreadful physical pain and worried about possible neurological damage, which nobody bothered to investigate. The authorities completely ignored the requests from James himself and from some European human rights organizations that had taken an interest in his case. The lack of medical assistance was so systematic as to raise the suspicion that it was a deliberate attempt to get rid of him.

James, in fact, was a thorn in the side of South Dakota's prison system. The state had previously done all it could to keep him in Marion federal prison, even after the twenty-two months of his federal sentence had expired. Why? Because Sioux Falls was still ringing with the echo of James's escape, that had taken place five years earlier. The press had christened the escape "South Dakota's Great Escape" and given it much attention in a way that had not put the police in a particularly good light. I heard this story from the European organizations that were trying to help James live long enough to obtain justice. Marjorie Tomkins, an American living in Italy who had founded an organization to help Native Peoples, was the first to write me about him. When her letter reached me, I didn't imagine that the solution to my quest to find a prisoner whom I had met months before in a dream was about to arrive by mail. I didn't know Marjorie. She wrote me because she had heard I was a journalist who had volunteered some work on human rights when I was still living in Italy. In light of this information, she thought I might be willing to lend a hand to gather some news about James' health. Her efforts from Italy had gone nowhere. Her inquiries with the prison authorities had never been addressed, and the requests of other supporters to provide James with basic medical care had been ignored.

I used to receive quite a bit of requests for help in those days. I couldn't answer all but there was something in Marjorie's letter that resonated with me. I decided to help however I could. I wrote a letter to the warden of the South Dakota State Penitentiary, explaining that I was a European journalist worried about James' health and that the press in my country was very interested in his case. The letter brought about a result that exceeded my expectations. Within a few days, James was given a CT scan: hearing that his brain showed no lesions greatly reassured him. Yet—as

James wrote me—more detailed tests were needed in order to rule out any secondary neurological damage as well as to ascertain the reason for his pain.

He also told me about how they had just thrown him into solitary confinement, in the ill famed "hole." He was shut up in a narrow cell, humid and dark, despite the precarious condition of his health. He wasn't allowed to receive visits involving physical contact—not even from close family members. However, prison policies allowed for an exception for lawyer visits, and for journalists.

"There are things, which for security reasons I cannot talk about neither by letter nor by phone. All my letters, coming in or going out, are read or copied. And the single weekly phone call I can make from here is always recorded."

Along with the letter, James sent me a photograph of himself. The picture hit me powerfully. Here was the same intensity of his gaze, his shoulder-length hair, the bandana on his forehead and the neck brace I had seen in the dream! An hour later, I had already called the prison warden to ask his permission to interview James. I had also booked the flight to Sioux Falls, the city where the penitentiary was located, about a hundred miles from the Yankton Sioux tribal land where James was born and raised.

The voice of the spirit comes in the most unexpected ways. It can come in great symbolic visions, like those that the Lakota and Cheyenne medicine men go seeking in vision quests, withdrawing from daily worries and confining themselves to solitary fasts, sitting for days in the same spot to invoke signs from the Great Spirit. But it can also take the form of a simple, tangible message, complete with a stamp and postmark. I have learned to recognize them by following my heart. The greatest lesson I have learned from my American Indian friends is that you should always follow what your heart is telling you. Rule Number One. For this gift, I keep giving thanks to the Universe. To give thanks for the gifts I have received. Nobody had ever taught me to pray in this manner in the Catholic churches of my childhood. By the time I turned ten, I refused to set foot in one again. In no school or any other institution had I ever learned that you don't pray to obtain, and you don't give to receive. But if you give with your heart, if you pray with your heart, the universe responds. In the old times, families used to celebrate the recovery of a loved one from sickness by throwing a big party and giving away everything they possessed. They were left without even a blanket to sleep on. By evening, though, someone would have brought them blankets, cooking pots, food, horses.

The Indian give-away ceremony is not a sacrifice. It is a celebration. Giving away is something you do with joy in your heart. What a splendid paradox to consider in a civilization like ours, based on possession and accumulation.

The capacity to foresee what the future holds by dreaming, sensing the possible dangers that lie in wait, is an ability I picked up as a child. I forgot about it when I was growing up. It came back all of a sudden, just like magic and in a totally natural way, since I began to connect to the Indian ways, a while before meeting James. And dreams have had a most important part in this story, often suggesting angles and solutions that my rational mind was unable to discover.

Ahò Mitakuye Oyasin!
In the Lakota-Sioux language, it means: "To all my relations!"

A Dakota Warrior

My name is James R. Weddell. I am thirty-nine years old, and I belong to the Yankton Sioux tribe of South Dakota. My people call themselves "Dakota," with a "d" as opposed to the "l" of the Lakota of the West. But we all belong, first and foremost, to the great Red Nation.

The Sioux were never a single people. Right from the beginning, they were divided into many bands. Among them could be distinguished three main groups: the Teton, the Santee, and the Yankton and Yanktonai. Each one of the bands called itself by the same name, which means, "allies." The difference lies in the pronunciation: "Lakota" for the Teton, "Nakota" for the Yankton and "Dakota" for the Santee. Our dialects reflect this difference, but today, for convenience, one speaks only of Lakota or Dakota. The white man gave all Natives the name "Indians" and the Lakota the name "Sioux".

The Sioux of the Great Plains were a proud people of hunters and warriors before the arrival of the white man. Our wars were different from those of the whites. A young warrior didn't need to kill in order to demonstrate his valor. It was enough to "count coup," that is, to touch his enemy – another Indian from a rival tribe – with the tip of a stick. Before horses were brought to the Americas, my people hunted the buffalo on foot. They disguised themselves wearing the hides of wolves so that they could approach without alarming the herd. And no buffalo was ever killed without first praying for its spirit, giving thanks to it for its generous sacrifice. From the buffalo, in fact, the grandparents of my grandparents took everything they needed to survive the harsh winters, when the raging blizzard blew and the snow fell in such quantities as to knock over the teepees in the camps. Blankets, clothing, and moccasins were obtained from its hide. Pemmican, which would sustain the whole tribe for months, was obtained from dried buffalo meat mixed with lard and wild berries. We made weapons and tools from its bones, soap from its marrow. In those times, when there were no enclosures for the animals nor reservations for us Indians, no one needed to sacrifice his dignity in exchange for government rations, good only to guarantee you a few pounds of white bread, salt, and canned food.

When the buffalo were deprived of the space needed to run freely in accordance with their nature and were almost wiped out, the Sioux ended up sharing the same destiny with the buffalo. We were deprived of our pride and our valor, robbed of the lands in which our ancestors had always lived, crowded into limited areas of bad land that the white man called reservations and forced to live there in captivity, just like cows in a fenced corral. We even underwent an enforced Christianization.

The whites, in fact, neither knew nor honored the power of *Wakan Tanka*, the energy of the universe that pervades and animates everything alive. Nor were they open to admit the existence of a god different from theirs, a god like *Tunkashila,* the Great Spirit, who has need of neither churches, nor priests, nor crowds of worshippers. Even our method of cultivation, offering prayers and nurturing the earth in exchange for its gifts through appropriate ceremonies, was for the whites a demonstration of ignorance and barbarity—something to be destroyed, rooted out just like our religion, our language, and our traditions. They even outlawed our most sacred ceremonies, like the Sun Dance and the Ghost Dance, which came out into the open again only in the 1970s. In those years, Greg Zephier brought back the Sundance to Marty, on my own reservation, following directions from Frank Fools Crow, one of the most respected Lakota medicine men. Before Congress passed the American Indian Religious Freedom Act, anyone caught practicing these ceremonies was persecuted. And they imposed the English language on us. In boarding schools, they would wash with soap the mouths of small children who were unable to express themselves in this foreign language and who continued instinctively to think and sometimes accidentally speak in Lakota. It is the children who have suffered, and continue to suffer from the theft of our culture. Even our names are no longer our own, since we were forced to adopt Christian names.

My Christian name is James. Jimmy, as my family calls me. Or Jim, as almost all my friends do, even here in prison. But for the elders of my tribe, for the traditional Sioux, I am Ista. This is my Indian name, which means, "eye". It's an abbreviation of Ista To'paicagopi which means "Square Eyes", and was given to me by a medicine man as a kid, or Wanblee Ista, which means "Eagle Eye." The latter was given to me by the chiefs when I was a young warrior, by Dennis Banks, who was one of the founders of the American Indian Movement, an organization that in the '70s organized resistance to our cultural genocide. I'm very proud of this name, because the eagle is the most sacred of all the animals. It represents the Great Spirit—

James receiving an eagle feather that Sam is tying to his hair, in 2003.

his enlightened vision.

It is the greatest honor to receive an eagle feather in recognition of one's own personal merits. I have received many over the course of my life. And even today, every so often, the prison medicine man brings me one that someone has left for me at the guardhouse. I have made a gift of some of my most sacred feathers to my Italian friends, who in these difficult years have sustained and helped me, fighting by my side without even ever having met me. And I sent one to Gloria for her birthday.

Women today are real warriors. Even in my tribe, if you want something done quickly and well, ask the women to do it. My mother and her mother, my grandmother Eliza—whose birthday was just a couple of days apart from mine on December 24—taught me to be who I am.

I am a warrior. A defender of my people. A traditional Indian who has not lost his sense of honor nor his spiritual values. I would never give them up for anything. I am the only one of my tribe who never accepted the money for the sale of the Black Hills, our most sacred land, which the Sioux consider to be the center of everything that is: the heart of Mother Earth from which all things come. The American government obtained them by means of an illegal treaty, and then tried to cleanse its conscience with a retroactive payment. Of all the Sioux bands, due to the actions of a corrupt and weak tribal government, only my tribe has shamefully voted in favor of that payment and broke the agreements established by the Intertribal Council.

I recall the desperation, the rage I felt when the checks arrived. It was almost Christmas, and I had no money to buy a present for my daughter Cicily, who was only seven years old at that time. I was sad and frustrated because I didn't have enough money for a Christmas gift for her, but I just couldn't use that money. There wasn't any reason good enough to betray my being a true Indian. I stuck the check above my bed with a thumb-tack and wrote on it with a felt pen: "NO WAY. The Black Hills are not for sale at any price."

I tried to convince my family and friends to support my stance. But weakness and greed got the better of them. My heart still bleeds for their betrayal.

It wasn't the first time that I had been betrayed. It's hard to be an Indian and keep your sense of honor intact. It's hard not to give into temptation, give into bribes. I'm aware of that. For that reason, I have always forgiven those who have betrayed, forgotten, and abandoned me. I lack the capacity to hate for longer than an instant. Resentment and vengeance are unknown to me. I follow, instead, the doctrine of my chiefs, the teachings of my elders. They have prepared me to always resist, even if I had to stand alone. And they taught me to conduct myself according to the Indian code of honor, forgiving and helping those who laugh at me and mistreat me. For this reason, I have been given a pipe and with it the responsibility that binds every pipe carrier.

A view of the Black Hills, from Needle Highway to Harney Peak

The pipe has been sacred to the Sioux since the earliest times, since White Buffalo Calf Woman came to bring the pipe as a gift to my people, so that through its smoke they could communicate with *Wakan Tanka*, pray for all the people and everything in the universe. That pipe still exists, handed down from generation to generation and guarded by a caretaker as the most sacred of our treasures. Many other pipes have been modeled after it, carved from the red stone of the Pipestone Quarry, which is located in our territory. If you'll ever have the honor to share the pipe with a traditional Indian who invited you to smoke it with him, your life will suddenly change. The Buddhist monks, I read, reach the same result with meditation. We use the pipe but it is the same prayer. When we smoke, we open our heart and feel all the beauty and harmony of the Universe, of the divine ordering of things. Wounds, disappointments, frustrations can be cured by that inner peace, which gives you the capacity to accept your destiny whatever it might be, and at the same time, renews your strength and will to fight for true and universal justice.

This is my story. It is what happened to me since I received my first pipe from the Raising Hail family. Since then, my wars have ended. I have pardoned even my jailers—even when they left me without tests and medical attention, to be driven mad by worries and by the pain in my head; even when they let a racist nurse try to poison me.

I am still a warrior. I always will be. But I am learning to use other ways of fighting battles in defense of my people. And even if in school, I didn't get beyond 8th grade, I'm learning the power of words. I've begun to make use of it even in arguments with the gangs here in prison, with the wildest and edgiest guys. I'm succeeding in persuading them to take a road other than that of violence. At times, I end up in trouble and my friends tell me, "Forget it, Jim. Let them stew in their own juice."

But that just isn't me. If I were like the others, someone who only cares about his own personal business and looks the other way when someone is in difficulty, I wouldn't be in prison today. But I wouldn't even be able to look at myself in the mirror in the morning, because I would have betrayed the spirit of Crazy Horse.

Crazy Horse was the greatest of all our heroes. He was as great as Sitting Bull, to say nothing of Dull Knife or Spotted Tail, who at the time of the Indian wars stuck their necks out despite the numerical predominance of the whites and the internal divisions among our people caused by corruption. If any of you come to South Dakota, go to the Black Hills and admire the mountain where his statue is being sculpted. Nothing like those big, ugly faces of the American presidents, roughly carved into the stone of Mount Rushmore! The statue of Crazy Horse will make them pale into insignificance.[1] He will change the course of history from that mountain just like he influenced the course of Indian history. He was one among our great chiefs who never signed a treaty. When Alvin Zephier, chief of the Yankton tribe in 1986, testified for the defense at my trial and stated that my actions and behavior were comparable to those of Crazy Horse, I wept. I am not ashamed to say it. I'm almost forty years of age and a warrior. But there are things that go straight to my heart and strike it like an arrow. Things that move me to the point where I cannot hold back the tears.

For that reason, it doesn't matter to me if they wound me, if they punish me or if they arrest me for having defended my own life or the life of others. I cannot recognize myself in the "justice" of the authorities. Can it be

---

[1] Crazy Horse Mountain is an on-going gigantic sculpture just a few miles from Mount Rushmore. Whereas the Lakota universally dislike Mount Rushmore and consider it a symbol of imperialism, they are more split about Crazy Horse Mountain. Some view any destruction of the natural environment of the Black Hills—no matter whether it is to honor a Lakota leader or not—as desecration. Others (James among them) approve of the project because they feel that a monument portraying Indians in a positive light is very important in a state with such a strong anti-Indian tradition.

right to allow an Indian girl to be raped by a bunch of drunken farmers at a party? Or else to allow your father, in a state of drunkenness, to be dragged out of a bar and beaten up, after he has blown his last cent on a drink? For this, for helping a terrified fourteen-year old escape rape, and for defending my father's dignity, they threw me in prison when I was still a young boy. Anyone who knows life on the reservations knows just how often that happens. How easy it is to be charged, tried, and convicted of non-existent crimes, if you do not have the money to get yourself a lawyer and the jury is an all white jury. This is contrary to the law. The law establishes that 15% of the jurors should belong to the same racial group as the accused, when he or she is a member of an ethnic minority. But if you are born in South Dakota and have red skin, the law isn't for you. It is never on your side. If Jesus Christ had been born an Indian in this place, he would have been put on trial, at the very least, for child molesting just for having said, "Suffer the little children to come unto me."

    You need to have had the experience of feeling different, feeling excluded and marginalized because of the color of your skin, before you can understand what I'm saying. Racism is the worst of aberrations—something I just can't understand, but also something that I've suffered from my whole life. In Scenic, a small and almost abandoned town in the middle of that spiritual arid land called the Badlands, there is a bar there, with a sign at the entrance bearing the writing: "No dogs and Indians allowed." By now, the sign has become almost a touristic attraction, but it tells the story of what it was like growing up an Indian in South Dakota, until not too long ago.

    My family name is Weddell. It isn't an Indian name like Black Elk or Lame Deer. I owe it to my great grandfather, Charles Weddell, a German or Scottish who moved to Vermillion in 1870 and then became the first white man to drive a stagecoach across our territory. He brought the mail to our reservation. On my mother side, my grandfather was a Norwegian, Oliver Thomas Gullikson. He fell in love with my grandmother Eliza, a real beauty, and her family adopted him without prejudice. My great grandfather Luke Red Bird's only request was for him to learn the Dakota language in order to marry his daughter. They called him Tom "Tall Fox". That was his Indian name because of his height, about 6' 5". My great grandmother, Eliza's mother, was Sarah Deloria. Her Indian name was *wah-check-kiya-wi,* that means "praying to God". She was believed to have died and come back to life thanks to her father's prayers.

So, in my veins, runs a bit of European blood, and I'm certainly not ashamed of it. That the races mingle and create new generations with mixed genetic and cultural heritage, seems to me to be a step on the road to better understanding. My skin is not quite as dark like that of the full-blood**s**. But in my heart, I am 100% Indian. Not like those we call red apples, red outside and white inside. They dress up in white man's clothes. They squeeze their necks into spotless white shirts with starched collars and ties, and they carry black leather briefcases, to look like whites. After being kept for five years away from the light of the sun, I am paler than a *wasicu,* a white man. But in any case, it's true that I belong to the fair-skinned side of my family. I am one of fifteen between brothers and sisters. Eight of us could have been the models for the Indian head on the silver coins, while the other seven have a light complexion and more delicate features. In some cases, they even have gray-blue eyes, like my brother Mike and my sister Rosie.

    I was born during the "moon of hard winter" in which the earth renews itself, in the depth of winter.

    I arrived on this earth right on Christmas Eve, and for that reason, my mother has always called me her little Christmas present, even if I was already the ninth of her children. We were six brothers and nine sisters: Benjamin,

William (Sam), Larry, me, Rodney (Ron), and Mike; Betty, Dorothy, Shirley, Marilyn (Mercy), Margaret, Mary, Eva, Rosie, and Carole. When we had to walk the nine miles to town to go to the public laundry, it took four of us to carry the bags with all our laundry! Children are sacred to Indians. They are indeed gifts from the Great Spirit. A large family is a blessing even when you are poor. This is another difference the whites cannot accept. Many of our women in the early 1900s have been sterilized without their knowledge in the clinics set up on the reservation by whites. "For their own good," of course. It happened, and still happens in some cases, to other tribal peoples, in Africa—for example. It is no great surprise. In these very same clinics, the pharmaceutical companies try out their new drugs before putting them on the market, using us as guinea pigs.

Anyway, in 1955, the year I was born, my family was poor—which was nothing out of the ordinary on the reservation. The rate of unemployment on our Res was close to 90% then, and the situation didn't greatly improve until the construction of the Fort Randall Casino, in 1992. The story of the Indian casinos is one that deserves to be told. On many reservations today, there are casinos run by Indians, whose proceeds go into the tribal coffers. Most states, in fact, don't want them on their lands, and they fought us trying to prevent us from having them on the reservation. But when it became clear that the law was on our side, they figured our casinos would fail in no time. But reality had some surprises in store for them. Among my people, especially among the new generations who have been able to study, there are excellent managers and administrators, capable of making investments pay off and transforming the earnings into new jobs. States continued to fight us by doing petty moves, such as trying to deny the Indian casinos' liquor licenses—a dirty trick that has fortunately been exposed in a court of law. My reservation didn't get a casino until 1992, and since then, the living conditions have greatly improved.

But during all the years before that, it was a very different story.

My father was an alcoholic, like almost all the men in those days. I don't condemn them for this. It's easy to fall into temptation when you go home in the evening and you can't even look your wife and kids in the face, because you haven't come anywhere near to finding a job, not even the most humble, with which to bring home money for a pair of shoes or a change of clothes for one of the kids. Without work, without social structures or meeting places apart from bars, without the comfort of the traditional values and strong spiritual beliefs of their fathers, the men fall one after the other into the trap of a glass of booze. It's the easy way to temporarily drown their sorrows, and forget the misery of their own existences, while dreaming of the ancient times, when a man could provide for his family simply by going hunting, and had no need for hand-outs from the whites.

In the course of the 1970s, when the Indian struggles against the government began again with the battles to win back the land and invalidate fraudulent treaties, the young Indians had the chance to at least recover a little of the old dignity that had been lost. But in my father's time, this wasn't an option. My father was never around. He was always off drinking some place, and when he was home, he was drunk there too. He would arrive in his 1936 Chevy, which had only one headlight and holes in the muffler, always announced by a loud clanging noise. If he was in a good mood, he would take us for a ride, all crammed into the old banger, and that was always a big occasion for us. I used to get into that car with great pride. It didn't matter to me that the headlight was broken, the paintwork chipped, the brakes missing and that two of the windows were made out of cellophane. With ten or twelve of us crammed in there, we never felt cold, even when the temperature dropped below zero. If you visit an Indian reservation, take a look at the cars. Many match my description. When they break down, no one has the money to fix them. And they break down often, due to the excessive loads they have to carry.

It is a typical Indian characteristic that—I have to confess—I am not immune from myself. For that reason, think twice if you're thinking of lending your car to Indian friends. If they come upon a family on the road that needs a lift, or they run into someone who has to transport a load of wood and has no other way of doing it, they won't hesitate to stop for them, in spite of what might be written in the instruction manual! Besides, for Indians the old saying, "Unity has strength," has always remained valid. Going around in a big group is a way of feeling more secure, and less afraid.

When I was growing up, fear was a fact of life for every Indian kid, particularly if you were little and weren't yet in a position to defend yourself. There is always some danger, some snare waiting for you. You are always being accused of having done something that provides an excellent excuse for punishing you. I remember a twelve-year old girl, a friend of mine, who went to jail for stealing a pack of cigarettes from a supermarket. And I remember too, the sheer terror I felt every single day, when I went to school and the white kids teased me, hurling insults and sometimes stones. I used to run all the way back home, without turning around or responding, just to avoid getting into trouble. Then one day, I couldn't take it any more, and I faced my assailant. He was twice my weight, and stood a head taller than me. But I was faster. Since then, I have never been afraid. And I have never backed down from a fight. If you can understand how I felt then—the anger, the sense of impotence at that unjust, inexplicable, and continuous persecution—you'll understand why my mother, when I was eight years old, came up to me and put a loaded gun in my hand.

"Use it to defend your life or someone else's life, Jimmy," she told me. And then she went on to tell me how you load it, point it, aim it, and clean it. Don't be shocked.

Mine is a checker-board reservation, where a great part of the lands have been sold to white people. And where there have always been white gangs going around to beat up or even kill Indians. They know that the police will probably do nothing about it, and choose instead to close their eyes without bothering to investigate. There have been mysterious cases of homicide filed away after the briefest of inquiries, whenever the victims had been Indians and the accused white. It has never happened the other way around. As with my case, in which one of the leaders of this gang, the Gregers, that had been terrorizing my people for more than fifty years, was killed in a brawl. I was accused and convicted even though there was no demonstrated evidence against me, and the pathologist changed his opinion on the cause of death at least three times during the course of the trial.

  I have never denied taking part in the brawl, nor have I denied striking Randy Caldwell in order to take away from him the police baton he was using to savagely beat an Indian boy. But I didn't kill him. His death was not my responsibility. They accused me in order to take me out of the way at an extremely delicate moment for "Indian affairs." I was one of the few remaining obstacles still standing in the way of the mining companies, the construction businesses and the pharmaceutical companies that were intent on exploiting my land and my people. One of the few left to oppose the destruction of the environment and the water pollution caused by these industries that care only about making a quick buck. And the only one, along with my brother Sam at that time, who still raised the Black Hills question in the tribal council, continuing to invite every kid who was about to turn eighteen not to accept those infamous checks.

  There are many ways of "persuading" an Indian protester to stop making trouble. You can set his house on fire—that's what happened to John Trudell, the Dakota poet who lost his wife and three children in a tragic house fire when he was far away and couldn't defend his family. You can cause mysterious accidents in which Indian cars are driven off the road by unknown people. The children of many leaders of A.I.M. have died this way. Or, again, you can fabricate trumped-up charges and throw them in prison to get them out of the way forever: as it happened to me, Leonard Peltier, and others. But we will always return. In this life or another. There will always be a warrior who is willing to fight for the Red Nation, as long as a single Indian remains. The Indians, as the ancient prophecy says, will exist as long as there will be buffalo. And the buffalo are growing back in numbers. There are statistics to prove it. The tribes are ranching them to repopulate our land with the animal we always shared it with.

I have never hunted a buffalo. No one from my generation has. I have hunted deer in the traditional manner, one against one, as was taught to me by my elders. It wasn't my father who taught me to hunt and fish. But I learned the rules and the prayers to be offered to the animals and the fish just the same. I learned to respect the animals whose lives you are going to take, as handed down in our traditions.

I have never killed for the love of it. I have never taken one life more than was necessary. When there was no work and no money, I used to get up early in the morning and go fishing in the Missouri River for the old people of my tribe who had no children, to put fresh food on their tables. At some point, my tribe had no money to take on a manager to restore the profitability of the tribal farm that had been brought to ruin and failure by the corrupt government. It was in that government's interest to reduce the tribe to a state of misery so that the tribal members would be "agreeable" to vote in favor of franchises that white companies wanted to establish in our territory. So, I volunteered my work. I knew nothing about harvesting, seeds, and tractors. I had to learn everything from scratch. And I worked for two and a half years without pay, living on what little savings I had managed to put aside. Now that there are funds in the tribal coffers, they could pay me for the work that I did at the time, and I wouldn't be forced to depend on the generosity of my friends in Europe in order to come up with the money for legal expenses. But up until now, they haven't done so, although I have asked them. It seems to me that when you go to prison, everyone forgets what you have done for them.

It doesn't matter. Like I have already said, I have been trained to resist even on my own and not throw in the towel. In my cell I have posted a sign on the wall that reads, "There is only one thing harder than resisting, giving up." That is the motto I have based my life upon. It's hard being an Indian, but I am proud to be one. And with the international support that has come my way, I know that my battle will be won, even in court. This time, I want victory even in the eyes of their law. Because the day that I will walk out of here as a free man, through the main gate of this prison (from which, if I wanted, I could escape like I have done in the past, in the face of all their security measures), will be a very important day. Not only for me, for the whole Indian nation.

For this reason, I grind my teeth and resist—to show my friends, my siblings, and their children that you can win, even against the state of South Dakota; to teach them to have courage and stand their ground, even when everything seems to be lost.

Encounter in Prison

May 28, 1993. It's cold for May, and the sky is overcast. The penitentiary, seen from the outside, is no worse than any other. It's an old red brick building—big, but not gigantic. As soon as you go inside, you can feel an unpleasant veiled threat that seems to stick like mold to the walls, the tile floor, the worn out chairs where you have to wait to be called by the guards, after presenting your id.

They seem to be alarmed by my presence. They check my driver license, and my journalist I.D. several times. They hold onto them and send me to sit in the entrance hall. After a while, they call me back to the guard's office and ask to check my tape recorder. They make a call "upstairs." No, I can't bring the tape recorder in. It wouldn't be of any use to me anyway, they say, because the visit will take place behind the glass, by intercom.

Why? I ask the guard. What about the right to confidentiality and freedom of speech?

These kinds of requests for basic prisoners' rights must be unheard of in South Dakota. In fact, a female guard passes next to me with a smug smile like the Cheshire Cat and hisses at me through her teeth.

"You're not in Europe here!"

Eventually, after being kept waiting for forty-five minutes, they call the visit for Weddell. To reach James, it takes another fifteen minutes. Fifteen minutes of doors that slam and electric barriers that take forever to open, of guards who search through my notebook and take my pen apart, who make me take my belt off my jeans, my earrings off my ears, my rings and bracelets off my fingers and wrists, my hairpin off my hair. Finally they dab some fluorescent paint on my hand and decide to let me pass.

James is angrier than me. Furious. He tells me straight up that a journalist from *Argus Leader*, a conservative newspaper from South Dakota, was able to meet him privately, in the attorneys' room, on the same day they brought him here. Apparently the prison regulations have different faces in South Dakota. Particularly where Indians are concerned.

Welcome to my country anyhow, James greets me, even if this is not the best place to receive a guest.

He has dark hollows and puffy bags under his eyes, and he's very pale. Even the blind could see that he isn't well. He has brought a whole file of papers with him, not realizing that he would only be able to show them to me through the glass.

It's a bad, cracking reception through the phone and the noise behind my shoulders is incredibly loud. I'm sitting in the same room where prisoners who are not kept in isolation get to meet their visitors, and are allowed physical contact with their family members. More than half of the faces around me are Native. The Indians don't amount to more than 10% of the total population of the state. In prison, these figures are reversed. More than a third of the prison population is Indian. They are mostly young men convicted of the most trivial offenses but with sentences that are on average double than those handed out to whites for the same crimes. James is in here for manslaughter in the first degree, with a sentence of eighty years, plus an extra fifteen added for his escape.

We start to talk about the most pressing subject, his health, and the medical tests that he needs but are continually refused. He shows me, across the glass, the weekly list of drugs that have been prescribed to him since his arrival. A disturbing chart, with doses of pain killers that would knock out a horse. A doctor who visited him recommended chiropractic treatments, but nobody followed up on his suggestion.

"The doctors of P.H.S. (Prison Health Services) usually do whatever the warden of the penitentiary wants them to do. They wouldn't dare defy his authority, because P.H.S. is a for-profit organization with a vested interest in maintaining its own economic position, no matter if it happens at the expenses of the most basic healthcare entitlement. The last doctor I talked with regarding my request for an M.R.I. left me in no doubt about this.

"Do you know—he told me—that an examination like the one you're asking for costs thousands of dollars?" Too expensive for an Indian, I guess. Therefore, the authorities put on the usual drill. The prison warden replies to the faxes from my friends of the human rights organization, saying, "I have to place my trust in the opinions of the experts."

"And the P.H.S. doctors, the experts, do what he expects of them, which is writing down anything saving him from having to spend too much of the taxpayers' money."

James has brought with him the medical records of other prisoners, hoping that I might be able to help them too. There's a boy from his tribe, Jim Red Fox, who has fallen in his cell and smashed his face in, causing paralysis to the whole left side as far as his arm. And there's a white prisoner who has full-blown tuberculosis, which could spread like wildfire in an environment like this.

"One day, this friend of mine passes in front of my cell, and I hear him coughing violently. I was making sage tea, so I ask him if he would like some. It could soothe your cold, I tell him. And he said, 'It's not a cold. It's tuberculosis.' I couldn't believe it, so he brought me the certificates to see. I have here his signature, which authorizes me to show them to you. But how can we go on with this glass? What time is it? Oh no, we only have five minutes left until they come and show you out. If we go on at this rate, I won't even manage to tell you how I ended up in here!"

I begin to get nervous too. I signal to the guard in his little room with bulletproof glass, and when he comes, I explain to him that it's impossible to conduct an interview in this manner. If they won't let me see James in the visiting room, they can at least pass me the documents. My pissed off yet balanced attitude must have convinced him since he decides to call upstairs. Partial victory. I can have the documents but only at the exit. First, they have to examine them one by one to check that James isn't passing me any secret messages. If he hands the papers over now, they will give them to me when I go back upstairs. James seems very worried at the thought of leaving his legal papers in the guards' hands. Therefore, I propose an alternative. I will take the documents up with me, and I'll wait for as long as necessary for them to be scrutinized. The guards are clearly irritated by my initiative, but they can scarcely refuse.

"Tell me what happened the day Randy Caldwell died," I suggest. "I can read the trial records another time, but I won't get another chance to hear your side of the story."

He closes his eyes and wavers for an instant. When he opens them again and begins to talk, it's as if I'm watching a film of the sequence of events that led up to his arrest.

"It was February 28^{th,} 1986. That day I woke up early and started working straight away. Joe Lovell, my partner in the construction company that I had just formed, arrived, and we drove from Wagner to Marty. We were going there to buy an old car so that we could take the engine out to replace the one in my truck, which had just blown up. We drove the car up to the house, and began the dismantling operation. It took the whole day. During the entire time, different people came to tell us that the Gregers and Randy Caldwell were beating up Enos Weston and J.R. Little, two young Indians.

Each time I suggested that they should report the matter to the police. Even when they told me that the police had ignored the complaint, I advised them to persist. I didn't want to get involved, not only because I had just created from scratch a company, that could be able to give work to many others from my tribe; but also because I wanted the police to do their duty. I had never resigned myself to the idea that some representatives of the so-called law and order have, in reality, an interest in stirring up disorder. "

"Around seven in the evening, we stopped working and decided to head for the pow-wow that was being held in Marty. The only problem being that we didn't have any transportation, as Joe had had to lend his car to his uncle. At that moment, Micky Honomichl showed up along with his brother Larry, and Jesse Costello. We asked them for a ride. As soon as we arrived in the center of Wagner, the Gregers began to follow us."

While James is talking, he looks at me straight in the eye. But at the same time, he keeps an attentive eye on everything that is happening at his shoulders, where other isolation prisoners take turns at the other two available intercoms. I understand the reason he was given the name "Square Eyes." I ask him who the Gregers are.

"They are an extended family of whites who have been beating up and terrorizing my people for more than half a century. Some of them have married Indian women and have had children with them, so now there are also Indians among them. They settled in Wagner when the Yankton reservation had just been opened up, buying up lots of land for a few dollars. The Gregers are bullies. There are some good people among them too, but they are truly few and far between."

"Tom Hartley, the police officer to whom the beatings taking place on that day had been reported, is a first cousin to many of the Gregers. He therefore decided that the situation was not serious enough to keep him from attending a retirement dinner. Loren Archambeau, the B.I.A. (Bureau of Indian Affairs) police officer, was not able to intervene because the Gregers involved were whites. The tribal police on Indian territory can only be involved in crimes committed by Indians. For crimes involving whites, there's the state police. And the state police that evening had a dinner to attend! It was no coincidence. The Gregers are useful to the state police for the purpose of intimidating the Indians. And the attitude of the state police is to let them get on with it."

"Anyway, as soon as we arrived in town, they began to trail us. Micky got out of the car. He wanted to ask them why they had beaten up those boys. The Gregers thought that we were hiding Enos Weston in the car, because Enos was a good friend of Micky. They made off without replying. We began to drive off again as well, but as soon as we arrived on the main street, two of the Gregers' cars tried to bar our way. Randy Caldwell was there, in his truck, and he pointed a 22 caliber rifle at us. We turned around and went to buy some gas. That's when we spotted J.R. Little and Scott Leroy. They were in such a sorry state that we could scarcely recognize them. They had been beaten up badly. We crossed the street and stopped in front of the liquor store to buy a few beers. All of a sudden, a mob of Gregers came out of the bar, saw Enos walking down the street and surrounded him. Randy Caldwell began to strike him hard with a police baton. Around him, he had about fifty of his friends ready to give him a hand. Enos, however, was on his own with nobody else ready to help. We decided that we couldn't just stay there and watch him be beaten to a pulp. I got out of the car first and went in. I took the baton from Randy's hands. As soon as I did this, I saw that Troy Greger was running towards Caldwell's truck. In the truck was the rifle that we had seen in Randy's hands just moments before, so I took off after him. While I was running, I turned around and saw that Randy and Enos were still fighting and that around them there were the Gregers, Micky, his brother

Larry, and Mike Weston, all jumped into the fight with clubs in their hands. It was very dark, and you could barely make out the silhouettes even from a few yards, but at a certain point I managed to see Randy Caldwell fall to the ground. Then everybody scattered, running in different directions. One of the Greger girls, Brookie Zephier, ran me over, together with her brother Terence. But at the trial, she lied and said that she had seen me on top of Randy, who was already collapsed on the ground, striking him four times. She lied, like other witnesses lied, witnesses into whose mouths words had been put by those who wanted me to be locked away. One of the girls, Michelle Picotte, even admitted having lied before the Grand Jury, but the appointed attorney put in charge of my defense didn't even call her as a witness at the trial!"

Marjorie Tompkins spoke to me, in her letter, about this attorney and his total, almost unbelievable incompetence and lack of experience. I ask James to go on with his story.

"I didn't have the money to hire an attorney privately, so the court assigned me Lee A. Tappe. He had always defended the Gregers, but I wasn't prejudiced. I still believed that someone who chose a profession like his would have to have justice in his heart above all else. I was wrong. When you get to read the records, you will be able to see for yourself what he did. He was an attorney, but he failed to take depositions from several people who had been present at the crime scene and who had offered to testify on my behalf. He didn't object, even when the pathologist, Doctor Randall, changed his deposition, after having clearly stated at the outset that Caldwell had died from a single blow to the left side of his head—a blow, which none of the witnesses had attributed to me. Dr. Randall decided to go instead for "a concert of blows" as the cause of death, so that more than one of us could be charged with the same crime. Lee A. Tappe didn't even challenge the exclusion of Indians from the jury, and when, after my arrest, I found out that permission had been given to a relative of the victim to sit on that jury, he refused to help me look into it."

James has raised several questions. Two in particular could have a crucial bearing on his application for a new trial. But time is pressing, and now we only have a few minutes left for quick messages. He tells me, however, that while he was in Marion, he carried out a considerable amount of research in order to find out the identity of this relative. He had written to the State Archives and even to the Mormons, who register all births and deaths, passing himself off as an orphan in search of his roots. But his research hit a snag. To continue sending him certificates, in fact, they asked him to send 500 dollars. He also tried to contact the renowned pathologist Doctor Vincent Di Maio, after seeing him on an episode of television show *60 Minutes* on CBS, in which Di Maio helped reverse the charges and secure the release of an illegal immigrant who had been in jail for seventeen years, wrongly accused of his wife's murder.

"When I saw Dr. Di Maio taking the side of this man whom everyone else had turned their backs on, I thought, 'This man has courage, and he certainly isn't a racist.' So I wrote to CBS, got his address, and wrote him my story, asking him if he would agree to review my case, and how much it would cost. I was pleasantly surprised when the doctor replied that he would look at my case for free and asked me to send him all my paperwork. I did so straight away, but that was the last time I heard from him. It might be that the transcripts never left Marion, that they were intercepted and blocked by the guards. It wouldn't surprise me. It happens to a lot of my mail, even here."

There is no one else left in the visiting room. I'm the last visitor, and two impatient correctional officers are waiting for James with handcuffs ready, outside the door of the little room beyond the glass. Another guard has already loaded onto his arms the file of legal documents that will come with me, and signals for me to leave.

"Everything is in those files. All my documents, my letters, the replies and the refusals that I have received in these seven years during which I have continued to fight alone, hoping to find a way out. If you find the time to read them, I'm sure you'll be convinced of my innocence. What I want is a new trial, ruled by justice rather than prejudice. A new trial would unveil the truth and expose the lies. When you go to my reservation and talk with my people, they will tell you the truth. They will tell you how things really are. And I know in my heart, that you will help me. The spirits told me long ago, 'Someone you never met will come from far away, and will help you regain your freedom.'

The Earth Keepers

I wrote a letter to the Grey Eagles and all the tribal councils of the Sioux Nation. Gloria, I want you to go meet them and deliver it in their hands. It speaks of the Paha Sapa, which in my language means Black Hills. It speaks of my tribe's regrettable decision to accept that blood-stained money. It's imperative that it reaches the Grey Eagles, who are the great inter-tribal Council of the Elders, reconstituted in 1988. Among them sit some of the wisest and most enlightened men of my people, Indians who have not forgotten what is the role of human beings: to respect and take care of Mother Earth.

Some people say that the famous speech attributed to Chief Seattle in 1854 was actually written by a white man. I don't know and ultimately don't care. What I know is that I agree with the sentiment. How can you buy or sell the sky, the warmth of the land? I concur with the idea that we are part of the earth, and it is part of us, that the lively water that moves in the streams and the rivers is not just water. It is the blood of our ancestors. But many don't see it this way. To them, one portion of land is the same as the next, and when they have conquered it and exploited it, they move on to the next. They don't see the earth as a mother but as an enemy. And so they treat it as something that can be bought, plundered, sold like bright beads.

From North to South, from East to West, there isn't a single Indian nation that isn't fighting a battle against the devastation the whites have made of the land, establishing military bases and conducting nuclear experiments, mining it to extract uranium or coal, poisoning the waters of the rivers, of the lakes and the seas. How deeply sad!

A long time ago I realized that, in defense of those who died in vain for the *Paha Sapa*, I would fight for the most sacred of the Sioux lands, the Black Hills. The American government annexed them to its territory illegally.

The Treaty of 1858 indicates that the Yankton sold much land west of the Missouri, but not the Black Hills.

And the 1868 Fort Laramie Treaty is even more explicit in giving us ammunition for the lawsuit undertaken by the legal representatives of the Lakota tribes. I have asked to be a party to this action for the recovery of the Black Hills in this very letter that I am giving you to be delivered to the Grey Eagles. My tribe has committed the most shameful act of dishonor by accepting that payment. But I want the Sioux to know that even among the Yankton there is someone who refused. And that many Yankton accepted without knowing what they were doing, without knowing what that money was really for. It is a shameful story that must be brought to the attention of the public. It's not a habit of the Indians to wash their dirty laundry in public, but in this case, I believe that an exception must be made.

A wicked action has been carried out towards my nation, as much from without as from within—politics, greed and dishonor being the conspirators. Mine is a nation that is dying, its sacredness has been betrayed, exploited, and sold off. The spirits of those who died ask for the understanding of the whole world. These unique individuals, bound together by their commitment and duty to the laws of Creation, stand for moral and spiritual responsibilities, and leave aside the laws of man long enough to permit their conscience to guide them.

I can feel them next to me when I pray facing South. At times, I even manage to see them.

I can see my chief, Johnny Stricker. Man, he was good! He taught me that the honor of the Indian nation must remain intact, even if it costs you your life. For this reason, even if I had to be the only one of my tribe to resist, I wouldn't sell the Black Hills, not even for a million dollars. I didn't do it when with that money I could have paid for an attorney to defend me at the trial. I wouldn't do it even if they offered me my freedom in return. There are things that are even more important than freedom. The honor of the Red Nation is one of them. The sacredness of the earth is another.

This is what I was thinking when I was given the responsibility to look after the medal, from the 1871 treaty [2] between my tribe and the United States.

I now entrusted it to my *kodas*, my Italian friends, for them to keep safe from the greed of those who might think of selling it as a historical relic, now that its value is known to be around 100,000 dollars! I always carried it with me, in my left pocket, like an amulet. When I was on the run and I slept at night hidden in ditches

---

[2] Gloria took care of the treaty medal for James until he was released from prison. In later years, James entrusted it to Bruce Allen, nephew of his wife Cindy, for safekeeping, knowing he would never sell it or allow anybody to do so.

or burrows, I held it tightly in my hand, and I felt all the blood spilled for those lands running through it.

I used to hear my ancestors crying, but I also heard their words of comfort and encouragement. I felt protected like I was wearing a Ghost Shirt, which our warriors used to wear for the Ghost Dance and which is said to have rendered them invincible and immortal, because bullets couldn't penetrate it. The medal has been worn by the most courageous men of my nation—handed down from generation to generation—and now the chiefs have chosen to give it to me. What greater recognition of his honor could a man wish for? There is no higher reward on this earth.

When my tribe sold off the Black Hills, I had not yet received the medal. I was inconsolable with shame. I was in prison, serving a five-year sentence for the Pork Plant takeover[3], when the matter came before the General Council.

1978 was a very sad year for us. On the 15th of July, the question was raised for the first time. The agenda for the General Council meeting was to reconsider the offer of monetary compensation for the Black Hills by the United States government. Ninety-eight voted in favor, and ten were against it. On the following 20th of October, the Business and Claim Committee postponed the General Council and the referendum ballot to the 15th and 16th of December. In the course of this meeting, the voting was divided into two parts, without explaining to the assembly what was involved.

The question was presented in a thoroughly unclear manner without reference to Article 2 of the Treaty of 1858, which delineates the ceded lands: no way does the description coincide with the Black Hills. But Larry

---

[3] The Pork Plant takeover was the occupation of the Yankton Sioux Industries undertaken by James and fellow political activists, after the plant manager had failed to address the Yankton concerns regarding hiring criteria, pay and working conditions.

Cournoyer, the most corrupt tribal president in the whole history of the Yankton, operated in such a way as to convince the majority of those present at the meeting of the legitimacy of the offer.

Also, it must not be forgotten that it was almost Christmas. And dangling the carrot of money just before Christmas was a deliberate act by those who wanted the motion to pass. They knew it would have been too much of a temptation in a poor country with an 89% unemployment rate. It's no wonder that the tribal members accepted. And it is also true that many Yankton didn't know where the money, paid on a per capita basis, came from, or what it was for, given that they lived off the reservation, and nobody bothered to explain it to them. When they did find out, it was too late. The checks had already been cashed and spent. When the checks arrived, honor became a secondary consideration to money. In the beginning, a fair number of Yankton turned it down, but they gradually melted away when the checks started to arrive. In the end, only my brother Sam and I were left.

I remember a sister of mine, whom I almost begged to refuse, telling me, "They will never give the Black Hills back to us. I have never heard of a scrap of land being given back to the Indians. So, you know that the best I can do is take my money while I'm still alive. You should take yours too."

600 members of the Yankton tribe were minors at that time. This meant that their shares would be held back until their eighteen birthdays. At that time, their decisions would be respected. But the same people who initiated the shameful events of 1978 attempted, during the 80s, to persuade the parents of the children to cash their checks and spend them on their education. At every meeting of the General Council, this proposal was rejected by a show of hands, after I had explained why it was wrong. In all these years, I have never given up on trying to persuade the young people not to accept that money. Every time, the parents

have labeled me a troublemaker and have told their kids, "Take the money while you can. Take the money like everyone else has."

I never even managed to persuade my daughter, my own flesh and blood. Everybody else was getting that money. I guess she couldn't resist peer pressure. I'm ashamed to admit it, but I am telling the story in order to get across just how weak my nation's honor is today, and just how strong is the bad influence that years of corrupt government have left us as a legacy.[4]

If I could succeed in persuading other kids to refuse their shares, that by itself would make this time I'm rotting in here worthwhile. It wouldn't matter to me at all if I had to languish longer, buried in paperwork and looking at the sky only from the same tiny rectangle, that fragment of basement window that looks out from my cell onto the courtyard.

Sometimes, I ask myself, is it possible that the Great Spirit has caused me to be caught and sent back to prison so that I could have the time to study and fight for the defense of the Black Hills?

Gloria, you have been in the *Paha Sapa*. You have hiked in the sacred heart of my ancestors' land, and you have felt their presence when you were walking on the deserted trails between the pines. The eagles came to greet you, because they knew what you were doing. They know that you have come to help my people. Help me to show the young people of my nation that they can still act like warriors. Help me to show them how the old ones would have acted in their position, so that the young ones can

---

[4] Many of James' nephews and nieces, and his daughter Cicily wish they never accepted that money when they turned eighteen, now that they fully understand the importance of refusing it. James' life-long battle for the Black Hills created this result, convincing more and more people to stand by his side.

restore the honor of their parents. Among the letters I have given you, there is one to the young people of the Yankton Nation. Ask Tim Giago to publish it on *Indian Country Today*. It is sold all over the reservations, not just in South Dakota, and it is the only national newspaper entirely run by Indians. At the time of my escape, it was called *Lakota Times*, and it was better then. More aggressive, more radical. It wasn't afraid to publish my letter when I was still on the run, despite the fact that in those days my picture was shown on T.V. The marshals had put me on their list of the "fifteen most wanted" and had put a bounty of 3,000 dollars on my head. Even some members of my family betrayed me, offering tip offs on my whereabouts. But the elders, the real Sioux, who often welcomed me in their homes, who hid me and fed me when my last hiding place was no longer safe, used to tell their children, "If you tell on Jimmy, I will disown you."

"Disown me from what? What would I inherit? We're completely broke!"

Those were their replies, lacking respect. And their elders retorted, "The inheritance that my father and mother left, and my grandparents before them: our Indian name, our pride, our traditions, our devotion to Mother Earth."

The elders knew. They knew that I had been one of the few to stand firm, to never give way on this issue. And they knew that I would not stop fighting to get back the right to take care of the lands of our ancestors.

Gloria... I know. I can get the Black Hills back. I would give my life to secure that goal. Help me. Help us to reach it. You and all the people like you who, even if they have skin of a different color, have a heart like that of a true Indian; a heart that bleeds for the wounds of the Earth. [5]

---

[5] From the very beginning, the Yankton relationship with the Americans proved to be different from the experience of other Lakota-Dakota tribes. Unlike the Teton and the

Santee, the Yankton always remained at peace with the U.S. government. In 1823, they helped the U.S. Army launch an attack against the Arikara tribe. They signed their first treaty with the United States promising to keep peaceful relations in 1815. In 1830, during another treaty they signed away to the American government 2.2 million acres of land in Iowa. In two amendments to the 1830 treaty, the Yankton gave up all of their land east of the modern South Dakota border. In 1851 several Yankton leaders, including Smutty Bear and Struck By the Ree, were among the many representatives of Plains Indian tribes to sign the first Fort Laramie Treaty, which acknowledged tribal sovereignty and promised annuities in exchange for guaranteeing safe passage for white settlers traveling through their lands.

  Lending an ear to the requests of land speculators who wanted access to Indian lands, in 1857 the Secretary of Interior initiated negotiations to convince the Yankton to give up much of their land. According to the plan, the Yankton would resettle on a smaller reservation in exchange for trade goods and annuities for many years to come. The man hired to convince the Yankton was Charles Picotte, the son of a Yankton woman and a French fur trader. In December 1857, a delegation of Yankton leaders went to Washington to discuss this possible treaty. The treaty was signed in 1858 under suspicious circumstances. While they were in Washington, the Yankton leaders were told not to drink water, since it was supposedly polluted, but only whiskey. When alcohol did not make all of them malleable enough to sign, Picotte proceeded to threaten those who held out until he managed to get their signature after months of harassment. Once the leaders returned from the east, many tribal members were outraged that the treaty had been signed without consulting with the entire community. This conflict erupted in a shootout in which Struck By the Ree, one of the leaders who was in favor of the treaty, was wounded by a faction within the tribe that opposed this agreement. As a result of this, the classic political split between a faction that was more than willing to accommodate American demands in exchange for money and one that wanted to resist American expansion took place among the Yankton as well. Despite the unhappiness among some factions of the tribe with the terms of the 1858 Treaty, and despite the tremendous corruption that characterized the conduct of the government agents in charge of distributing their annuities, the Yankton never took up arms against the United States. In 1862, this commitment to peace was severely tested. In that year, their eastern relatives, the Santee, decided to launch what came to be called as the Minnesota Uprising. Despite promises to the contrary, after they had agreed to give up much of their land and settle on a reservation, the Santee were forced into near-starvation when hardly any of the annuities they were promised arrived. Enraged, the Santee decided to fight and quickly forced the evacuation of the entire non-Indian population of the state. At the beginning of the uprising, they sent messengers to the Yankton asking them to join the fight. The Yankton were facing a similar situation since most of the money that was supposed to be used to provide for them ended up in the pockets of the reservation agent, but the tribe did not think the uprising would be successful. For this reason, the Yankton refused and the Santee were ultimately defeated.

White Justice

Today, I received a letter from another prisoner incarcerated in Sioux Falls. Tony Rios, a seventeen-year old Lakota boy, in jail since he was fourteen for defending himself against an unprovoked attack by a white man.

I had read about his case in the library, while I was researching data on the different sentences given in South Dakota to people of different races convicted of the same crimes. It appears that Tony was in the company of an Indian woman whom he hadn't known long. They were chatting in her car in a supermarket parking lot. The woman told him that she had just left the man she lived with, a really abusive and violent guy who kept her away from her friends and beat her.

At a certain point, the woman got out of the car to go buy a couple of drinks. While she was away, a man came up to the car and forcibly dragged Tony out of it. Tony didn't have the least idea of what was going on. He only understood that the man's intentions were anything but friendly. In fact, he was hurling racist insults at him, and began to hit him without any reason. The white man, who turned out to be the guy the woman used to live with, broke the Indian boy's little finger and told him that he had done it so that it would stay bent in a "C," as in the initial of "Custer"[6]. Then pulling the boy's t-shirt over his head, he

---

[6] The famous army officer George Armstrong Custer, who prompted the expedition that led to the theft of the Black Hills, and who was killed by the Lakota at the battle of the Little Big Horn

continued to rain blows on him. Tony was blinded by the shirt but succeeded in getting a hand free, and instinctively reached into the back pocket of his jeans, where he kept a pocket knife. In a state of panic and with the sole intention of stopping the attack, he waved his knife around blindly. Misfortune had it that the knife struck a vital point in his attacker's abdomen.

The man slumped to the ground. Tony immediately called for help, but when he saw that, along with the ambulance, the police was arriving too, he fled. He was afraid of the police. His mother, Thelma, was and is an activist in the American Indian Movement. Their home in the Lakota Houses—a project on the east side of Rapid City—had often been the scene of raids, searches, and gratuitous police violence. Tony was tried before a tribunal for adults after having spent five months waiting in a correctional institution where he tried to kill himself more than once, afflicted by the distress and a sense of guilt resulting from that senseless death. At the trial "witnesses" appeared who had never been seen at the scene of the crime. They gave a version of events that painted the young boy as a hardened criminal. His family had no money to pay for an attorney, so they assigned him an appointed attorney who did all he could to side with the prosecution. The chance to shut Thelma up and make her give in had finally presented itself on a silver tray.

Tony was given twenty years for first-degree manslaughter and sent to serve his sentence in a prison for adults. Of course, as soon as he arrived in the SDSP, he was beaten up and sexually assaulted. The only intervention by the prison authorities was to throw him in the "hole" for trying to defend himself. Since then, he has been in the hole all this time. They have just let him out, thanks to the protests of his supporters. They formed a support group that is trying to get the money together to pay for an attorney and get his case reopened. Tony's life in prison has been an uninterrupted nightmare, which has only increased his depression and pushed him to make further attempts at suicide. His mother Thelma has had to sell everything she owned to pay bribes to the same gang of prisoners who had victimized him, so they would leave him alone and protect him from other gangs. She even sold her car, so she has not been able to visit him, which would involve traveling the distance of 350 miles between her house in Rapid City and the prison in Sioux Falls. In three years, Tony has only had a single visit from his sister and brother-in-law, who are the only ones who have managed to put together enough money for the trip.

    The prison guards call him "redskin" and keep provoking him. Tony is young. He doesn't have the capacity for self-control that others who are older and more experienced have. So, he is largely unable to tolerate the vexations and frustrations of prison life.

    Tony isn't the only case of a minor imprisoned at Sioux Falls. There aren't any whites among them, though. Just Indian boys. In other states, where there are no Indians, it's the black boys who end up in the prisons for adults, or the "brown" Mexicans. There's a judge in Aurora County, South Dakota, Judge Boyd McMurchine, who in the course of a few months, has sent to prison seven Indian boys between fourteen and seventeen years of age. They had escaped from the correctional unit in which they were serving sentences for minor crimes. I ask myself how a judge can bring himself to send to a prison for adults a young kid whose main crime has been to run away. I wonder if this judge has children of his own, and if he has ever thought that something might happen to them.

    I have received letters from other Indian prisoners, and they all confirm that the treatment they receive is much harsher than that reserved to the white prisoners. Even the medical treatments are administered on a racist basis, as demonstrated by the doctor who refused to prescribe James the M.R.I. test on the grounds that "it costs too much." Warren "Magic Turtle" told me that when he fell and sprained his knee, he couldn't stand up without the help of a knee brace. It was a Saturday. The doctor wasn't there. And even if he had been, a month could have passed between the request and his obtaining a visit. He decided to talk to the prison nurse. All that was needed was a simple knee brace. The nurse said that there were none available. Then a white prisoner, a friend of Warren's, went to ask the same male nurse for one pretending that it was for himself, and managed to get it.

  Iron Moccasin wrote me about how he and other nine prisoners were subjected to disciplinary action for refusing to take down some religious images from the wall. There were only two Indians in the group, and they were the only ones to end up in the "hole" for a month. I don't find it hard to believe. The first time that I visited a prison, a female guard in the visiting room came up to me as I was leaving and asked me, almost with disgust, why I was helping "the redskins." The notion that a white woman could take their cases to heart simply made no sense to her. From the following visit onward, she began calling me, "Gloria of the Indians," pointing me out with disdain to the other guards. I smiled at her and looked her in the eye. I even thanked her for that name and said that I was proud of it. From then on, she never spoke another word to me. But as soon as she was in a position to do me harm again, she seized the chance. She told lies about me to the prison warden, so that I was denied the chance for a face-to-face meeting with James, without glass partitions or intercoms, despite my then recognized status as "attorney assistant", something I had worked very hard for. It's obviously not easy to work on a case without the opportunity to record what is said and exchange confidential information. She was aware of that, but didn't care.

Racism in the prison system reflects the blatant racism that is endemic in the judicial system of South Dakota. During these months, I have examined the cases of various Native American prisoners who have been charged with absurd sentences, thanks to the principles of a double-faced justice system.

The most sensational and infamous case is that of Leonard Peltier, victim of a shameful conspiracy, as Peter Matthiessen has shown in his book, *In the Spirit of Crazy Horse*. Leonard has been locked up since the 1970s, guilty only of having helped his people. He is serving two life sentences in the federal prison in Leavenworth, Kansas, for a crime for which no one, not even the FBI with all its stratagems and tricks, has been able to prove his guilt. The story dates back to 1975. Two federal agents died in a shoot out during a police raid on the Pine Ridge reservation—a raid that was part of the government's campaign of revenge after the occupation of Wounded Knee[7]. That day, another man also died. But he was an Indian and therefore no one bothered about it. The death of an Indian certainly cannot be compared to the death of a white man in the eyes of the judicial system of South Dakota. Everyone was firing, and Leonard had a rifle too. The shots that killed the agents didn't come from his gun. Leonard, tough, was a recognized leader, a warrior who stood in the way of the government's plans. Those were years of terror on Indian reservations in South Dakota. The American Indian Movement, successful in promoting a new renaissance of the Indian spirit, was hated and feared like the Black Panthers by local rednecks.

---

[7] During the 1973 occupation of Wounded Knee, over 300 American Indian Movement members took over the site of the 1890 massacre of hundreds of Lakota people at the hands of the U.S. Army. The occupation gave high visibility to the government's failure to uphold the treaties it had signed with the American Indian tribes throughout its history.

What a great opportunity to pin the blame for those deaths on one of its leaders!

When an Indian is a defendant, prejudice is a simple reality. Poverty is another element in his disfavor, since the so-called appointed attorneys assigned by the court to the Indians seem to be handpicked for their inefficiency and state-of-the-art professional incompetence. Defense attorneys who "forget" to call favorable witnesses, who make the motions to separate the trials of the persons accused of the same crimes when the time to do so has already expired. Defense attorneys who do not insist upon the presence among the jurors of a 15% quota of persons belonging to the same racial minority as the accused, and who acquiesce instead, letting their Indian client be judged by a jury composed exclusively of whites. Defense attorneys who advise their clients to plead guilty even when they are innocent. And then you have judges like Judge Kern, who have already drawn their conclusions in their heads even before the hearing begins, on the simple basis of previous convictions, without knowing anything about the circumstances leading up to them. And let's not forget forensic pathologists who put their signatures on autopsies they haven't even carried out in person, and who release statements convenient to the prosecution often taking direct clues from them.

Dr. Randall, the pathologist in charge of the autopsy in James' case, issued three separate, mutually contradictory opinions at different stages of the trial. To start with, he decided that Randy Caldwell had died from a single blow to the head, on the left side of the jaw and the neck. Then he changed his story when the prosecution became aware of the fact that the fake witnesses who had testified that James had hit Caldwell in the head had stated that he hit him exclusively on the right side. This was an unacceptable lack of precision for a doctor who had had the opportunity to carry out all the analyses necessary on the body of the victim. On the left side of the head, on the scalp, there were clear marks left by a metallic weapon—probably a car jack. And the witnesses had agreed in saying that James had held only a wooden baton in his hand—which would have ruled it out as the killing weapon. But Randall maintained that it wasn't possible to establish the nature of the lethal weapon. His incompetence wasn't challenged by Lee Tappe, the attorney assigned to James' defense.

A few days ago, the daily newspaper *Argus Leader* reported that a case in which the accused had been sentenced to life in prison, on the basis of Dr. Randall's testimony alone, had been re-opened. Randall had thought it over, a year later, and had decided to change his opinion.

Throughout the United States, there are about 400 qualified forensic pathologists, who hold the qualifications to carry out an autopsy for a court case. What happens in reality is that often the person who examines the victim is only an assistant or else a general practitioner. The result can lead to innocent people being given life sentences. It has even happened from time to time that the pathologist whose signature appears on the autopsy report has not even left the airport of his city of residence, more than a thousand miles from the morgue, as has been brought to my attention by Dr. William Eckert, the founder of an international society of pathologists that offers help in controversial cases.

Ernestine Perea, accused of having shot his wife in the back, was sentenced to life in prison. When the CBS television show *60 Minutes* decided to investigate his case, a journalist was sent to the house of the pathologist who had sanctioned Perea's conviction. Samples of blood and urine from a case were found in the kitchen next to ketchup and jam. And among his professional credentials, they discovered the case of a man who had had his spleen taken out many years before: and yet the good doctor somehow managed to record the weight of the non-existent spleen in the autopsy report.

Peter Matthiessen has brought to the attention of the American public the story of a case that is just as scandalous. In 1976, close to the time of the shoot out at Pine Ridge that led to Leonard Peltier's imprisonment, the lifeless body of a woman was found. It appeared to match the description of Anna Mae Pictou Aquash. Anna Mae was a young A.I.M. leader and was extremely active in defending the rights of Indians. They found her frozen in the woods, dead for at least three days. Dr. W.O. Brown, the pathologist from the hospital in Scottbluff, Nebraska, where the corpse was taken for the autopsy, concluded that the only wound noticed was a small bruise on the head. He also stated that he was ruling out any possibility of sexual violence, despite being clear that the woman had had sexual intercourse a short while before dying. He decided therefore that the cause of death was that she had frozen to death, and he filed the case away as normal and routine. The strange thing was that Brown, the same pathologist to whom the government had turned over other mysterious Indian deaths, always obtaining reassuring results, decided to cut off the hands of the cadaver at the wrist. In order to justify this irregular procedure, he later maintained that he had done so, because given the advanced state of decomposition, he hadn't been in a position to take fingerprints himself. He had preferred to send them to an unspecified FBI agent.

Anna Mae's family was informed of that discovery by A.I.M. activists. When they arrived for the identification, the body had already been buried. Offended at the lack of consideration shown by the forensic pathologist, and not trusting his findings about Anna Mae, her family obtained an order for the exhumation of the corpse.

They had a strong suspicion. Remembering that Anna Mae had spoken, in her last days, about feeling threatened, and close to retribution for her "revolutionary" activities, they demanded that a second autopsy be carried out by a doctor less compromised by involvement with government agencies. In a few minutes, Dr. Garry Peterson, a pathologist from the hospital in St. Paul, Minnesota, discovered that Anna Mae had been executed pure and simple. They had shot her in the back of the head at point-blank range, and the bullet was still lodged in her head. Dr. Brown had not even bothered to carry out an X-ray examination while he had not hesitated to amputate her hands before anyone could realize that this was the corpse of the A.I.M. activist. It was also found that Anna Mae had very probably been raped, a very common fate, in those years, for Indian girls on the reservations—particularly when they were A.I.M. sympathizers.

In James's case, the pathologist's performance was not the only irregularity. By chance, one of the trial transcripts got lost, the only time this has happened in the whole history of the court in Charles Mix County. It was in fact the transcript of the grand jury in which that girl, Michelle Picotte, retracted her testimony for the prosecution, admitted that she had been given instructions by the Gregers on what she had to say. Also the videotaped statement of James's co-defendant, Micky Honomichl, disappeared. In the video, Honomichl stated that James had struck Caldwell on the right. Lee Tappe didn't even ask that the videotape be produced along with the other evidence. Attorney Tappe's masterstroke, however, came next. When at the end of the trial, James was informed of the possibility that a relative of the victim had sat on the jury, Tappe tried to convince him that this was of no real importance and that there was no point in following it up as a possible grounds for appeal.

For years James has tried to shed light on this matter on his own without any help, impeded by all the difficulties involved in being locked up in prison and being without financial means. I got angry when I read the hundreds of letters and questionnaires that James has sent from Marion to the South Dakota State Archives and even to the Mormons, to get hold of those simple pieces of information that his defense attorney would have been able to provide him without any difficulty.

I have also felt a great sense of admiration thinking about the courage, the faith, and constancy that James has managed to maintain in the face of continual refusals and consequent disappointments.

We have now organized a worldwide fundraising campaign in order to pay the legal fees for a good attorney. It was James who chose him. "Terry Pechota is a Lakota—he explained—A fighter, a democrat in a reactionary and conservative state. I know that he will not give up until he will succeed in getting me a new trial. And, besides, he only takes on those cases that he knows he can win."

Hopefully, Terry Pechota will.

On The Run

Of all the things that the guards, the prison warden, and all his ass-kissers say about me, there's only one that's true: I am an escape artist. In all of South Dakota, there's no one who has escaped from the slammer as much as I have. And every time, as the sequence of events has shown, I had good reasons. This is why the spirits have protected me, helping me go away with their permission and escape punishment that I didn't deserve.

The first time I escaped I was fifteen years old. The reason they sentenced me to juvenile detention was this: I was at home with my siblings minding my business, but someone came to knock on our door telling us that our father was getting beaten up in the middle of the street. One of my brothers and I ran over to see what was going on, and sure enough rumors were right. The typical scene that plays out every time Indians run out of money in a bar was being repeated here. My father had gone drinking in a bar owned by non-Indians, the only one in town. As soon as he run out of money, they kicked him out but the bouncers got a bit overenthusiastic about making sure he wouldn't come back in. Beating the hell out of drunken Indians was a form of amusement for them. So, by the time we arrived on the scene they were still hitting him while he was on the ground. We didn't take that too well, and promptly got into a fight with them to defend our father. We pummeled them and threw one of them through the bar windows. The end result? Juvenile detention, here I come. Ironically enough, the detention center was located in the Black Hills—my first experience of my people's sacred lands was incarceration!

By the time I arrived there, I had already decided that I had done nothing I felt ashamed of, and was not in the mood to accept punishment for that. So, before nighttime came I put my clothes in the dryer since I knew I was in for a long, cold night. As soon as they were warm, I snuck out into the yard taking my first step in my career as an escape artist. My first step on this path was almost the last since by the time I reached a fence where I had seen a small hole I couldn't find it anymore. It was getting dark and I began panicking. Right in that moment, I saw a deer across the fence. He was completely unafraid, just a few steps away, staring at me. He got even closer until I was able to touch him through the fence. The deer took a few steps away but kept looking at me as if he was making sure I would follow him. He walked along the perimeter until he came to rest just at the spot where the fence was damaged. It was as if he were guiding me. I dug under the fence making the hole bigger until I could squeeze through. I was free! And, on the run. I barely had time to celebrate that the floodlights hit the fence, an alarm rang and guards came out looking for me. They had already noticed I was missing. Adrenaline filled my body and I was ready to run, but the deer again looked at me and slowly walked off inviting me to follow him. I followed the deer through the night and the guards never found me. I truly believe the deer helped me get through my first escape.

Even now, if I wanted to, I could sneak out of here, passing beyond these cement walls and that barbed wire to which I don't belong. The oldest prisoners, those who know me by reputation, make bets on my escape. There's one, in fact, who has put 10,000 dollars on it, so sure he is that I'm about to run away. I said it loud and clear to the press as well, the day they picked me up the last time: if the Great Spirit didn't want me behind bars, there wouldn't be a state penitentiary nor a federal prison capable of holding me.

But this time around, I have listened to another voice. I have made a commitment. I know that now, thanks to the international support I have received, I will get a new trial in which all the lies will be exposed, and I'll be free to walk out of here by the main gate. That day will be a great day for the whole Indian nation.

My only concern is to stay alive until that date. The hatred of the prison officers and the big shots is still so strong towards me, for having made a fool of them that they would stop at nothing to prevent me from walking out of here. This is not paranoia. A little while ago, two nurses tried to poison me. They gave me "medicine" that made me so violently ill that I had to drag myself across the cell floor, from the bed to the door to call for help. And a week later, I heard from two different prisoners that certain prison administrators had offered them freedom in return for "bumping me off." I have no reason to doubt the word of my two companions. I don't even know one of them. I wouldn't be able to pick him out in a line up. Lucky for me, he wasn't the amoral son of a bitch willing to kill for his own self-interest that my jailers hoped he was. Both of them even declared themselves willing to testify in court, named the individuals involved in plotting my murder, and described in details the plan that had been devised to eliminate me. The idea was to beat me to death in a deserted corridor behind the Coca Cola machine after having lured me there with a false certificate of admission to the hospital. I felt a shudder running all down my spine when I noticed that the soda machine had already been moved into the position that my informers had described. This is just their style. The same cowardly tactics of the killers of Crazy Horse, who had invited him to discuss the possibility of a better reservation for his people, but instead were planning to have him arrested or killed.

The feds and the bureaucrats who sit today at the most import desks in this and other prisons are the spiritual descendants of General Custer and the other folks who came to conquer us. But we have inherited the blood-stained shirt of that great Indian chief, and we have decided to resist in his name. Deception, lying, sneaky tricks: these are the battle strategies of those people, when open persecution is not enough. Leonard Crow Dog, the medicine man who more than anyone sustained the warriors spiritually during the occupation of Wounded Knee in the '70s, knows something about that. Even before he was born, his father Henry, a great holy man and spiritual leader, was punished for refusing to submit himself to the religion of the Catholic missionaries. He was chased out of his home in the settlement of St. Francis, forced to wander with his family, on foot, and without destination, during a terrible storm: an experience that Leonard's newborn brother didn't survive. Leonard's sister, Delphine, was beaten up by the B.I.A. police, the Indian police in the pocket of the American government, and abandoned in a field where she froze to death. His nephew Andrew Stewart was killed at the age of eighteen by an "accidental" gunshot while he was in the company of a policeman. And when Leonard was in prison, where he served twenty-seven months before the false charges against him were set aside, the house of his elderly parents mysteriously went up in flames. It burned to the ground in the space of a few hours. It was only by a miracle that all the occupants were saved!

Like I said, this is their style: sneaky traps, vile and hideous tricks. They don't have the courage to fight in the light of day, one against one, in the manner of warriors, nor to allow justice to be truly justice and let it take its course. It is not the truth they seek. Their purpose is the same as that of their predecessors who came to ruin our existence centuries ago. Their guiding principle of that time remains valid, "the only good Indian is a dead Indian." Or else, a "good Indian" can be segregated behind bars, without power and without hope, reduced to silence and submission. Or else again, he's good as long as he joins their ranks, and works in their service in exchange for a handful of privileges, with the illusion of being able to nibble at the leftovers from the table of the famous American dream. That's a "good Indian" who deserves to be tossed a bone.

The only reason I would consider escaping now is to avoid their cowardly plots. A warrior does not have fear of any tangible adversary who presents himself in full sight. You need to have had the experience of fearing for your life in an abnormal environment like a prison to know what it means. I have received the order from my chiefs to go on resisting and never give up, even if I have to stand alone, and I will never fail in my duty. But like Yankton tribal member Judy Kalkowsky said in front of the camera during the shooting of the video documentary on my case: "Where there is no other way out, the warrior's duty is to escape from the enemy camp and go back to his people." This has always been the Indian way since time immemorial. It is the law of my nation, and I will certainly not be the one to break it.

Don't misunderstand me. I don't wish to escape. If there is one thing that I really don't want, it's to go back to living on the run, continually pursued and hunted like an animal, without peace and without the chance of actively helping people. But if I had to realize that I was too close to death, if I felt that cold breath already on my neck, I would want to die free under the open sky, breathing fresh air for the last time. Therefore, if today I speak of escape, I talk about it only as if it were the one chance I had left to preserve my life, without any alternative. And if my escape were successful, I would immediately surrender to whatever other country might be willing to guarantee my safety until the day of my trial.

My word of honor is not something I give lightly.

When I escaped from here in '87, nine months after my conviction, I fled out of desperation. I had been betrayed by many, convicted after a farcical trial in which I practically received no defense, separated from my friends and family, and no one had come to my aid, and no one was going to afterwards. I had no money to pay for a lawyer. I had no legal way out. So I escaped.

It was '86, and I had just got here, when they gave me a job in the mechanical maintenance workshop. Everything was repaired there, from school desks to televisions, from radios to recording machines for the blind, and we also built Christmas toys for the children of the most disadvantaged families. I used to work with two of my cousins plus other eight inmates. Our boss was one of those guys who minds his own business—a circumstance that was much to our advantage. He used to assign a job to you, and then he went away, leaving you in peace to get on with it. He was a good boss—I have to say.

The months passed. Christmas came, and I was still getting by. Then spring came, and I began to feel more and more uneasy. I became withdrawn, sad. I had made myself a very high chair, from which I was able to look out of the window. The view wasn't the best. I could only see the granite wall, but it was better than just looking at the inside of my cell. So one day I was sitting on my chair and I was praying in silence. I asked the Great Spirit if he could help me to win back my freedom, because I was the only one whom I could count on to gather the evidence in order to demonstrate my innocence.

Absorbed as I was in prayer, I didn't hear him coming in. He put his hand on my left shoulder and said: *"Tonska,,* nephew, don't take it bad, and don't worry. You are about to go home, much sooner than you think. You shouldn't be here. So pray. I will return."

It wasn't the Great Spirit in person, but it was he who spoke through the prison medicine man. Richard "Brother of All" is from my tribe. His name alone says a lot about the character of this man. Like it happens to a lot of my people, even Richard wasn't immune from the temptation of drinking, and this got him a bad reputation, even among the prisoners. But I had also heard a lot of good things said about him, and I wasn't prejudiced. It had been said to me that at one time, he had conducted a lot of *inipi*, the sweat lodges in which the Indians purify themselves before ceremonies, and that he was a singer of sacred songs. And also that he had always tried to help, through prayer, whoever might ask him. Therefore Richard is *wakan,* holy.

I finished my prayers and went out into the yard. I was speaking with my fellow inmates when Richard returned.

"Nephew," he said. "This is a piece of tree bark. Tell me what you hear." He cupped his hands to my ears. THE BARK WAS SINGING! He passed it around us all, cupping his hands to their ears as well and asking the same question. But the others laughed at him. Richard didn't get angry. He looked at them and said only this:

"You must believe."

I knew what I had heard and so I believed. He looked at me. There was determination in those clear old eyes. He said: "*Tonska,* four days from today, you bring eight pieces of white cloth cut in squares to make tobacco ties."

Then he walked towards me, and I heard that he was singing the same song as the bark. When he reached me, he said:

"Remember, the Great Spirit is everywhere, even with those who don't believe in him. *Doksa,* goodbye, in four days you finish the drum."

He touched my left shoulder, and when his eyes met mine, it looked as if he were sucked up into his mind. His last words were "four days," and he went away. When Richard had left, my companions began to laugh and make fun of him. Even so, I went to get the drum that I was making for the White Swan Singers, a very talented Yankton group, and I began to stick the pieces together. One of them said:

"Did you see his eyes?"

I began to laugh, someone else had seen and heard the same things as me, but was too weak to admit it. They asked me why he had come, and I told them. But I didn't tell them what the *pejuta* was for, the medicine that Richard had instructed me to prepare. When work was over, I went back to my cell and washed. I was drying my face when I felt something strange, that sensation you feel when someone is watching you, even before you see them. In fact, Richard was there again, right in my cell.

"*Tonska,*" he told me. "Certain people don't like me, but that doesn't bother me. I was an alcoholic and so there have been many rumors about me. Us Indians grow weak when we drink. This is the reason why your companions make fun of me, even though they are also my nephews. However, I have come to tell you to fast for these four days. I will fast with you. *Doksa,* for four days." And he went away.

The fourth day came. As he had instructed, I took the pieces of white cloth that I prepared to make the tobacco ties with me when I went to work, and Richard arrived mid-afternoon.

"O.K.," he told me. "Now tie the prayers, putting a lock of your hair in every square of cloth, along with the tobacco. We will bury four of them here in the courtyard and the other four you must send home."

So we buried the first four. We prayed, and Richard said, "Tomorrow these will be gone."

It seemed impossible, because no one goes into the yard after 3:30 in the afternoon, and none of the guards had seen us bury them. But on the following day, the tobacco ties were really gone. So when the weekend came, I gave the others to Evelyn[8] and told her to hang them up in our bedroom, like Richard had told me.

---

[8] James' first wife, mother of Cicily

Evelyn and James, at the time of this story.

Four days later, I was walking next to the repair shop, and I heard two white brothers talking about escaping. I went over and said to them, "I'm coming with you." At first they tried to put me off, then they seem to reconsider, realizing that I could help them. They had a plan, but it would have brought us out right under the guard tower. So I suggested sawing through a few extra bars, bending them back every night up until the time would come for the cutting to be completely done, and get out through the ventilation ducts. We sawed bars for three months.

One day during that period, Richard, who knew nothing about what I was doing, said to me, "A little longer, and you will be free. Don't drink alcohol or you will be captured. And from today until you leave, eat just one meal a day. There is just one other condition. You will have to be with nature, and if you do so, everything will be fine. Remember, *tonska*, they will offer monetary rewards for your capture and even those closest to you, will betray you. Don't hate them. They are weak, and they have forgotten the Indian spirit because of all the temptations around them. You prepare a medicine bag, put it in your left pocket and never let anybody touch it."

Richard knew! Everything he had said had happened up to that point.

I prepared a pouch like the one that I have now made for you, wrapping sage and sweetgrass from a Sun Dance in deerskin, along with bitter root and buffalo hair, the colors of the Universe and of the Four Directions, a lock of my hair and flesh offerings, little squares of skin cut from my left arm. In our religion, in fact, to make a prayer stronger and to get it answered, one offers his own flesh, just as the dancers do in the Sun Dance.

May 27th arrived, and the days of fasting paid off! When it comes to squeezing yourself into a tiny passageway all smeared with Vaseline, having semi-fasted for months comes as a great help! Six of us broke out in what the papers called "the biggest escape in the history of South Dakota." Others were supposed to come with us, but they got scared at the last minute.

We separated right away. It wasn't appropriate to continue to make our escape in such a large group. I stayed with the only other Indian, Ron Horned Eagle, another Yankton like me. It seemed logical that we should make for our reservation together, a distance of about a hundred miles from Sioux Falls.

Naturally, the prison authorities didn't take it too well. In a few moments from the second they realized that a breakout occurred, their agitation turned into a deployment of forces on an incredible scale. Horned Eagle and I fled toward the East, but when we arrived in sight of the river, we had to stop and hide ourselves in the trees. There were eight police motorboats in the water, and a number of helicopters in the sky such as I had never been seen before. The sky was clear and blue, and it wasn't a good omen. Our only chance of slipping through their net would be a storm. So I told my companion to take his medicine bag out of his pocket, and pray.

We prayed to the Thunder Beings, facing toward the West, because it's there that they live. All the storms come from the West. In a few minutes, a great black cloud appeared right over the penitentiary. It began to rain hard, so incredibly hard that the motorboats and the helicopters had to leave. We were starting to freeze, sitting there motionless and soaked to our bones, so we began to walk up the ravine. On its edge, we found a sleeping bag, which had been abandoned there and was miraculously still dry. I cut it in half, making two ponchos out of it. We took our shirts off, and we hung them out to dry. In fact, even if the sun was going down, the sky was clear again. We prayed, and this time the fog came to our aid. A thick fog protected us for the next three days during which we ran and walked almost non-stop. We slipped across the roadblocks until we arrived at the eastern border of our reservation. We were eight miles from my house when we heard the drum. My friends, the White Swan Singers, were singing my honoring song. The words were naturally in Lakota, but the translation goes:
>Indian boy, get up on your feet,
>It is hard to be an Indian,
>Get on your feet Indian boy,
>It's real hard to be an Indian.

It's an old song from the 19th century. That day, Evelyn and my mother asked the medicine man to come and pray for me, to help me with their prayers and protect me while all the marshals and the federal agents were hunting me down.

    For weeks, we lived along the banks of the Missouri River, hiding ourselves in the tunnels that we dug in the crumbly soil. The sheriffs, the B.I.A. police, and the federal marshals, all of them were after us. One day, when I was out looking for food, I found them hot on my heels. I ran down a ravine so fast that I could have broken the world speed record. I came to where the trees grew thicker, and I took advantage of them, digging a hole right there. I had to stay all crouched down for four nights and five days. When I got back to our hideout, my companion was gone. Tiredness, tension, and fear had got the better of him, so he had decided to give himself up to the police. The others who had broken out with us had all already been recaptured. They were captured within forty-five days. I stayed out for two years and three days.

    For most of the time, I stayed on Indian land, on my own and other Indian reservations. But the newspapers went wild, inventing fantastic sightings in California and Florida. One time, someone was able to lend me a Kawasaki 750 motorbike, and I managed to get away from South Dakota for a while. More often than not, I slept under the stars. To keep up my spirit, I sang myself the words of that country song, the one that goes:

> I am a friend to the thunder
> Is it any wonder
> lightning strikes me
> and I'm no stranger to the rain,
> I was sacrificed by brothers,
> crucified by lovers,
> but through it all,
> I withstood the pain.

It seemed to fit my situation perfectly.

At times, I was forced to ask for help, but I tried to avoid it as much as possible. My family and friends were being put through a lot of trouble because of my escapee status. My brothers were being followed, having their cars stopped on their way to work, with guns pointed to their heads, to see if I was hiding in their trucks. My mother's house was being searched regularly. One of my sisters, Marilyn, whom we call "Mercy", was arrested on a charge of having tried to "extradite" me while she was on a trip in East Florida. The principal of my daughter Cicily's school gave her a hard time when a little boy who was her friend showed up in school wearing a t-shirt with "Free James Weddell" written on it. In short, my escape was already causing them enough problems without me thinking of making more trouble for them.

Fortunately, the elders were on my side. They seemed to be competing with each other to offer me their support in every way. One day, it was the 31st of October, Halloween, and I remember it like it was yesterday. I went to a party with a mask on my face. Winter was fast approaching and the weather was getting rough, like only South Dakotans know how, with blizzards blowing at a hundred miles per hour and snow covering cars and houses within a few hours. I didn't stand much of a chance of surviving if I didn't find shelter. On that night, when everybody else was still partying, I walked to an elderly woman's house and asked her to let me in. I showed her the letter stating that James Weddell was one of the very few who had refused the money for the sale of the Black Hills, and made some comments on the fact that the marshals had just offered a reward of 3,000 dollars for his capture: "In a few days, he will be alone, with even his flesh and blood ready to give him up for that money", I told her.

It was then that she said to me, "Bring him here and I will help him. He will be safe with me."

I took off my mask. When she recognized me, the woman started to cry and hugged me tight. I kept this story secret for many years until this great, courageous friend of mine, a real Indian whom I had the honor of knowing, told me to go ahead and tell her story. "What can they do to an old woman warrior like me, a grandmother?" she said.
The marshals and the B.I.A. officers used to come over at her house and ask her if she had seen me, and she would offer them coffee with me right under them, hidden by a trapdoor, listening to them. How we laughed about that, afterwards! Even now that I'm back in prison, she is with me and keeps supporting my cause. I can feel her presence together with my mom's, my family, my friends and the spirits of my chiefs. It is their presence that helps me to put up with this life in here, which isn't worth living.

However, in spite of Marshall Gene Abdullah dedicating his whole existence to my recapture, I got caught for only two reasons. The first was that on the 22nd of September in '88, the marshals put me on their list of the "The Fifteen Most Wanted Men in America."

I was the first and only man from South Dakota to appear on that list, and I was in the company of the worst criminals in the nation! On October 16th, the Fox television network transmitted the list with photos. By that same evening, their headquarters in Washington had received forty-four telephone calls that reported having seen me here and there. It's incredible what egomania television can feed in people's minds. I began to feel the breath of my pursuers on my neck. I even thought about crossing the California border to hide myself in Mexico. I thought I could fit in there, we look somewhat the same, but I didn't know one word of Spanish. It was during those days that I decided to dip the ends of my fingertips in boiling oil to destroy my fingerprints so that it would be impossible to identify me, should I be captured. I don't recommend it! The pain is unimaginable, almost unbearable.

Meanwhile, in all post offices throughout the Mid-West, wanted posters were hung, displaying the reward on my head. But I wasn't yet in their trap. If I had stayed camped out in the Black Hills, in the sacred heart of my nation, I'm sure that not even the best trained men from the federal services and the police could have tracked me down. However, I made a mistake. I broke the vow I had made when I promised Richard that I wouldn't drink.

It was the 29th of May 1989, and I had gone with some friends to a concert on the Pine Ridge reservation, the "Battle of the Bands". I was so frustrated thinking about those who had let me down at the time of my trial and betrayed me for those wretched 3,000 dollars that I began to drink whiskey and soda. All I wanted was… to forget my thoughts; to forget myself completely and let the music fill my head.

At 6:30 the next morning, on the return trip, the Pine Ridge tribal police began to stop cars because of an accident that had happened in a nearby campsite. I was sleeping in the back seat, but as soon as I heard my friends get out of the car, I leapt to the wheel and tried to make off in the direction of the Kyle dam. In a few seconds, police cars appeared from every direction. I tried to hide myself under water, but there were fifteen men combing the area inch by inch. So I had to surrender. It was the Indian police themselves who captured me, who succeeded where the feds and the sheriffs with their unlimited resources had failed.

My capture provoked indignant reactions from the Indians. I still remember the letter to *Indian Country Today* from Darwin Apple, a reader from Springfield: "The spirits of our dead will cry tonight", said his letter. "Because they cannot accept that it has been the Indians themselves who have committed this act of infamy, handing over one of our own to the marshals."

There was no obligation for the B.I.A. to hand me over to the marshals. They could have simply arrested me and handed me over to the reservation judges, claiming the right of sovereignty. However, I wasn't from the Oglala tribe of Pine Ridge, and unfortunately, divisions and rivalries exist even among Indians. So they gave me a summary trial and added fifteen years to my sentence. Now, it stands at a total of ninety-five years.

For good measure, they dug up an old story. When I had been arrested in 1986, I was given probation for illegal possession of a firearm, carrying a sentence of twenty-two months for that minor offense. On Indian reservations, everybody carry guns for protection, and I wasn't going to walk around unarmed just because they didn't like to allow me to care for my own safety. Anyhow, they revoked the conditions and sent me to Marion, in Illinois, one of the toughest prisons in America. When the twenty-two months expired, the state of South Dakota contracted with the federal government to keep me there. Illegally. Had it not been for the campaign of letters, faxes, and telephone calls from my *kodas* to the governor and even to the President, I would still be in Marion. I recall a judge, Judge Kern, who was so blinded by his hatred that he made the mistake of writing to Valeria, a supporter from Florence, Italy:

"Why do you want to help James Weddell? You might consider him a hero, but he is only a punk criminal with a crime record longer than all the legs in your group."

If Judge Kern had taken the trouble to cast an eye over my record and the circumstances of my offenses, maybe he would have learned something. I'm not a murderer. I have never used physical force other than in defense of myself and others, and never when I could avoid it. And the greater part of those so-called crimes were political acts like the occupation of a factory. Every time, I have been tried and sent to prison. At times, I have escaped, in order to demonstrate my innocence.

The truth is that when an Indian is charged, you can be certain that he will end up behind bars, guilty or not, and he will have a hard time getting out. This is because of how the law is carried out in South Dakota, and this is the reason why most of the time our families forget us, when we get arrested. An Indian is already given up for dead in court, the same moment his guilty verdict is read.

But I've never been scared of being left alone. I have my faith, my spirituality, the energizing power of my conviction. If you believe in what you are doing with all your heart, you can do anything. I believe this to be true. That is why, perhaps, the spirits are helping me.

Dreams and Visions

I came to visit you last night. You were sleeping with your jaw contracted. I slipped past the bars and the bolts, as light as a cloud. The guard sat dozing in his chair. I touched your hair. You look younger with your forehead uncovered, without the bandana.

Someone cursed in a cell further down the corridor. On the table, there was a letter addressed to me, left unfinished. I took a peek only at the first few lines.

You are always amazed when we manage to find each other in this way, as if you didn't believe it possible to dream together.

The first time I thought that you were about to have a heart attack.

"You were here with me!" You told me on the phone, choosing your words carefully. You asked me take off my neck brace… and you were massaging my neck and my shoulders… and you showed me the points to press to reduce the pain… and in the morning, I woke up, and THE COLLAR WAS HANGING AT THE FOOT OF THE BED!"

I smiled at your incredulity. It's not that difficult to dream this way. You give yourself a simple, precise goal. Then you concentrate all your intention on that purpose, and pray for it to come true. Mine was to let you know that you weren't alone; to embrace you, in defiance of those glass partitions; to help you get better without medicine. If I had been able to touch you, massage you like I was shown by my Chinese qi gong masters, the energy which was stagnating in some points of your body would have begun to flow again.

Illnesses are generated from blocks that exist, first and foremost, in our minds. Blocks created by the magnetic storm of our emotions when we are not in equilibrium. And how can you be in balance, terrorized and cut through by anxiety and pain?

So I came while you were sleeping, flying away from my sleeping body and passing among the stars. I guess you felt my energy in your sleep, despite the absence of my physical presence, because you "woke up."

You heard me, and listened to me. You watched what I was doing, and learned. And you smiled. I had never ever seen you smile that way. A child's smile, all bright eyes filled with amazement.

Since then, you have flushed the analgesics down the toilet. Less risky. If they really want to make attempts on your life in the most shameful manner, let them pour the poison into a glass of champagne!

Since then, dreams have been our special time for talking and listening without guards around us, or phone recordings. Without gates, bars, and handcuffs.

We discuss secret strategies and share little intimacies in our dreams. In the aboriginal language, there is no difference between life and dreams. The same word is used for both of them.

You were an ant in one of my dreams. An enormous ant, all black and gold, that had come to teach me patience. Not one of my virtues.

I was ill in those days, from a strange and sudden "illness." I could scarcely breathe. It was as if I had a rock on my chest and someone was crushing my ribcage in his arms. My temperature had gone up to 104. It prevented me from concentrating or understanding. I tried to figure out the causes of that illness so that I could cure myself, but I couldn't. My mind wandered, unable to focus, and my frenzy was growing. I was unable to appeal to calm or willpower. I was overwhelmed by the unclassifiable symptoms of that unknown virus.

My dreams later revealed the mystery of that ailment that was swallowing up all my energy, and I recovered the strength I needed to start fighting again.

My rebirth gave you new strength, just like I felt my own strength grow from seeing you regain control over your pain.

At times, I would prefer not to feel everything that you feel. It's too painful. But most of the time, I am grateful to this telepathic link that we established between us, right from our first meeting. It is convenient to have a private open line of communication when one of the two of us lives in a prison.

It is not just telepathy. Our thoughts and feelings ride on the same wave, something that goes beyond what can be explained. Who knows? Perhaps we really did know each other in another time, another life. But I don't recall it.

For a long time, in my dreams there has been another Indian. He is very old, with long, thick hair like a mantle of snow on his naked shoulders. He is old, but his body is powerful and muscular. He rides with the pride of a young warrior. He almost always rides a white Appaloosa flecked with gray. With him, I always found myself among the wolves and in caves. He taught me to dance with snakes and to fish for salmon in the manner of the bears, catching them with bare hands. He told me his name, but doesn't want me to reveal it. He has come, he says, to teach me how to help. He came long before I came to you. Even before I came to live in America.

That time, I dreamed that I was in the Black Hills. I had visited them during a trip I took some years ago, but this was the first time that I had dreamed about the *Paha Sapa.* He entered my dream ripping open the sky and clearing a passage for himself in the blue background. He appeared in front of me with that piercing, searching stare of his, and he didn't speak. Then, he beckoned me to follow and we began walking towards the peak. I couldn't resist his summons. But neither did I want to. I trusted him instinctively, like you trust your grandfather when you are a child. I perceived his wisdom and his power. And I was happy that he took me with him.

He took me to a place where other elders were sitting in a circle. The elders instructed me to move the energy inside my body in a special way until I felt a fire building up inside me. They told me that with that fire, I could cure myself and cure others of all ills. I believed it, because the warmth that I felt developing in my arms and hands was immensely pleasing. I had never experienced anything like it. And I could use it, they told me, to call for a dream every time I was in need of answers.

Sometimes, I don't even have to call. The dreams arrive and light the way like flaming arrows burning in the night sky. Do you remember when I told you that we had to fast together for seven months, the first four days of each month?

It had never been a very clear dream. It was linked to the moon and to its cycle of twenty-eight days. My Indian friend had taught me to divide up the cycle in that way, promising that it would bring a positive result. I was a little hesitant when I told you about this. We had only known each other for a couple of days, and I didn't know how you would react. We hadn't had the time to talk about dreams. I didn't know if you believed in their messages. I hadn't even told you that it had been a dream that had brought me to you.

You didn't ask for any explanation. Your grandmother Eliza and your mother Hazel had taught you, when you were still in diapers, that the world is governed by dreams, by portents and omens.

"Our day began around the fire, telling each other about our dreams. First those of us children, all light and color. And finally, those of Grandmother, symbols and prophecies. It was our theatre."

The Huichol Indians who live in Mexico in the western Sierra Nevada have always shared the same morning ritual As soon as they get up, they gather together, sitting in a circle on the beaten earth floor of the hut. In the center, in a hole, a fire is kindled. And to Tewari, Grandfather Fire, they confide the visions of the night. Little splinters, fragments of an unconscious knowledge that are translated into premonitions and prophecies for daily living. It is dreams that regulate even sowings and harvests, as it was in ancient civilizations.

The tribal cultures have kept that wisdom. They have not forgotten. Among the aborigines of Australia, there is no cure for healing that can possibly work if it has not been first dreamt. The shaman meets the invalid. He touches him. He listens to him. He smells him. He makes no diagnoses and offers no remedies. That would be impossible before dreaming. The dreams will tell him what that particular ailment has been caused by and what herbs, what roots to look for in order to cure the sick.

The tribal medicine men of other traditions also cure this way. With inspiration and imagination. And the patient, in the end, recovers through dreaming that he is well.

We began to fast on the first day of June, as the dream told us to do. On December 14th, a few days after we had completed the seventh fast, the letter came from Dr. Di Maio. His opinion exonerated you.

If dreams didn't exist, neither would the Sistine Chapel exist, nor would the capacity to give form and realization to the world of imagination. For some time now, a date has kept recurring. It appears to me on calendars hung on the walls or else the headlines of newspapers on which the year is printed, and it is always 1996. It has become almost an obsession. I ask myself what that date is trying to tell me. Will it be the year of the new trial?

"If only they would grant me a hearing and agree to consider the new evidence that we have uncovered in our months of research," you said to me. "They could even dispense with the formality of a trial. Any judge at all could see that I am innocent, and that going to court would only be a waste of the state's time and money."

Delusions, James. These are the dreams that never come true.

How can you imagine that the State of South Dakota would let you go easily, without a fight?

Instead, they'll pull out all the stops. They will turn down our application. They will refuse both the hearing and the trial, allowing the legal time limit to expire before giving us an answer. But when that time is over, we will not despair at the State's intransigence, and we will go to the Supreme Court. And there, we will be heard.

Because I dreamed it to be so. And dreams do come true for those who fight to realize them. [9]

---

[9] Gloria's dream proved to be prophetic. A hearing before judge Rush was obtained in September 1995, where the new evidence was presented and James testified for twenty minutes. A verdict was expected for spring 1996. It took instead eight more years for James to gain his freedom, and it happened only through the last possible stage, before the Federal Supreme Court.

International Solidarity

Today I found out that Micky will be let out on parole next year—this coming after they have already cut his sentence by a third. The same people who have decided to commute the punishment of my scatterbrained companion, have refused to even consider my application. In some way, this intransigence makes me feel stronger. I would never lower myself to plead for their mercy. How could I express remorse for a crime I didn't commit?

It would appear logical that I should be able to walk out of here as a free man as well. But their justice is never logical. Obtaining freedom through the proper channels is the greatest of my ambitions, and at the same time, the most difficult of my goals. Who knows if I'd have the same strength to hope and endure, if I didn't have all these new friends to sustain me?

With you at my side, it is as if I had a fire inside me—a fire in my heart that warms me inside. The elders, my chiefs, the medicine men, predicted it for many years. "Fire is coming," they said. "Someone whom you don't know, whom you have never seen in your life, will come to help you."

No one, no one but myself, could understand what this has meant and how much it still means to feel all these people around me who think and care about me, without ever having met me. I was used to fighting alone, to suffering injustice when I could no longer resist, and to pay the price of my battles while not many cared. From the time I was recaptured, even most members of my family seemed to have given up on me. In all the time I was in Marion, I rarely received letters from them, and never a visit. I have thirteen brothers and sisters who are still alive, and around 300 nieces and nephews. But not one of them in four years has ever acted on the urge to get down there. I can count on my fingers even the ones who have come to visit me here in South Dakota, just a hundred miles from their houses. When I asked, they said it breaks their heart to see me here. What about my heart? Don't they realize how much a visit can cheer me up? How long after that I can still feel the energy from those visits? How much it keeps me going?

    I can't complain, though. I have had the honor of receiving some of my Italian friends like Marco, Antonia, Marina, Marjorie, Michele, who have flown 10,000 miles across the ocean just to smile at me from the other side of a glass partition. Stefano and Osvaldo have in fact given up their vacation and invested all the money they have saved to travel to my reservation and help Gloria make a documentary on my case. We didn't know each other. We had never even written to each other, and yet they have behaved like my own brothers by blood!

    I feel no resentment towards my family. I love them just the same with the same intensity, and I do not blame them for their neglect. Perhaps the impotence they feel, and the fear of standing up to the State, have prevented them from helping me on an emotional level and even from expressing their affection. I know that they remember me in prayers and ceremonies, and that feels good. I am sorry that they don't understand that more displays of their affection would be enough to make me feel that I am still alive in their hearts. But I'm sure that it will change, now that they will regain hope, seeing how Gloria will be able to reopen my case. The day I will get a new trial, I know they will all be there for me.[10] Feelings are the only wealth of someone who

---

[10] After the September, 1995 hearing, James' family recovered hope that he could indeed regain his freedom. They came around, wrote more and paid him some visits

has lost everything. When you are locked up counting the hours and even the minutes, pacing the same few square feet day in, day out, a letter or a photograph can give you back the scent of the earth and the warmth of denied embraces. One day, I asked my mother to send me a photograph of the fried bread that she used to make like no one else in the world. I savored that photo to the last mouthful! And I breathed the sparkling air and the spray from the waterfalls in Yosemite when Daniele went to camp out there. I could feel the Spirit of the Earth in all my cells, when photos arrived from my *kodas'* trip to the Black Hills. Every time that one of you sends me a thought, a photograph or even a wish to share your joy and your feelings with me, tears of emotion fill my eyes! At times, I ask myself what I have done to deserve all this.

Someone will think that I'm crazy to say this in my position, but I am sincere. I consider myself fortunate—blessed in a special way through the international solidarity I have received. Sometimes, I even think that it is for the best that all this happened, or else I would have never had the opportunity to meet you. I have never met people like you Italians in all my life.

Almost all the whites I ever had to deal with before were mean to me, with very few exceptions. The whites with whom I grew up on the same land made me weary of them

---

before he left South Dakota again. In fact, in December 1995, Gloria obtained him a transfer to the Montana State Penitentiary, in Deer Lodge. There James was not only safer but also no longer segregated. Contrary to the South Dakota policy in his regard, he was admitted to general population, allowed to have contact visits and work as a gardener on the prison grounds. He started running ten miles a day during recreation periods and regained his color back. It wasn't freedom yet, but definitely improvement of his living conditions.

by hating me just because I wasn't like them. They hurt me just for the pleasure of hurting me with a cruelty that I could never understand.

I remember one incident in particular. It was in 1981. I had just been released after having served a term of imprisonment for the occupation of the Pork Plant, and I was going to visit my grandmother, who lived in the old peoples' houses on the reservation. One of her sons, my uncle, who lived with her, kept a dog tied to the front door. It was a huge white Labrador that never stopped barking, not even for an instant. My uncle told me that he was going to have to kill him. The dog woke the old people up at all hours of the night, and many of them had already complained. If he didn't kill him, they were going to throw him, my grandmother, and the dog out onto the street.

"I would bark too if I was chained up all day with no more than eight feet to move around", I told my uncle to persuade him to treat the dog more decently. But he repeated that he was going to kill him. Therefore, I took the dog away with me that same night.

I put him in the car, on the passenger seat. As soon as I sat on the driver seat, the dog started licking my face. He seemed to know that I had saved his life. I spoke to him. I told him that his name was King. He understood, and looked at me in that characteristic way of his that made him appear almost human, leaning his face to one side. I never kept him tied up. In fact, I let him sleep in the house, stretched out across the hallway. No one could come to knock on the bedroom door without King hearing him first. The children adored him, and King went to meet them at the stop when the bus brought them back from school. He was proud to be their protector. Whenever I went to fish or cut wood for the old people, King would come with me. The first time that he saw me with an electric saw, he growled and tried to stop it, thinking that it would do me harm. I had to explain to King how it worked before switching it on again. I have never had a friend that I could trust like that dog. I felt safe with him. I was 100% certain that he understood me.

One day, King disappeared. The children announced this to me when I came home from work. They were very agitated. They said that a police officer had come and had taken King away. I knew that guy, so I went to see him, and I asked why he had taken away my friend and where he was. He denied knowing anything about it. A couple of days later, some friends arrived from a nearby town and told me that they had seen King with a police officer. The officer had made King get out of the car into a ditch, and had shot him in the head. I searched in all the ditches in the area, but I never did find King. I was mad. I cried with anger. I thought that police officer had to really hate me to a truly incredibly extent to make him murder my friend so viciously! But I never did find out why he did it. However much I tried, I have never figured out just how a man can hate to a point of committing a mean action like that. I'd done nothing to that police officer. I only knew him by sight and reputation. I knew that he was a racist, but I never would have imagined that meanness and ignorance could have pushed him to such a cruel act.

I am a simple man. My education is limited. My culture is the earth. I grew up on a reservation and its boundaries were my horizons. I used to work hard from dawn to dusk, and I had no time for reading or vacations. In the evening, I would stretch myself out laying directly on the dirt, feeling the dampness of the earth with my back. That was my vacation. I used to lose myself among the stars, and I would listen to the music of the creatures of the night. That was my way of working off my tiredness, and replenishing my energy. That was my daily meditation, taught to me by the earth. My people have always found comfort in nature. A man in the midst of nature is never alone because he has the animals, the rocks, the trees, and the rivers for friends.

It's impossible to feel sad when you feel the presence of such wonder around you. The energy of Creation enters inside you and won't let you feel isolated anymore, closed up in your own shell with your big problems. You feel yourself at one with the Whole. That feeling of wholeness and unity is what I miss most from the times when I was free. It is difficult to feel that way when you are enclosed in four cement walls, with heavy iron bars to reduce your sky to a squalid little square, letting you wonder where the sun or the moon can be. Far from the winged brothers and the four-legged ones, separated from the life that runs in the water of the streams. But the cosmic magic of the Universe has managed to give me back what had been taken away from me so brutally. Nature and feelings have re-entered my life like a hurricane, sweeping away walls and bars, coming with your messages. Smoke signals from countries that I never even knew existed.

You know that song by Johnny Cash? "Love is a burning thing, and it makes a fiery ring, bound by wild desire, I fell into a ring of fire...." Ring of Fire! In secret, that's what I call you. It is the Indian name that I have given to you all, new brothers and sisters of my extended family that now stretches as far as Europe. When I met you, all I had left was my dignity. All else had been stripped away from me. You have given everything back to me. That "everything" which, in our tradition, is said to be born from the Black Hills. That everything which is at the origin of existence, which is the very essence of life. To feel part of *Wakan Tanka* again is enough to help me to get by. I will never forget it, and one day when I'll be free, I will help you. I live for that day. What might I do to return all the energy your affection has rekindled? To give back twice what has been received, which is the Indian way? Man! No human being could give to another more than what you have given to me. It was Christmas 1991, when I received the first letters from Italy. Christmas Day was no different from any of the other days that I had already passed in Marion prison. No letters, no visits. Holiday periods are the hardest for prisoners. They reopen old wounds, which makes you more vulnerable. They increase the longing for people and places. It's easy to fall into despair and feel forgotten. On December 26th, I tried to force myself to recover my spirit. My grandmother Eliza was born on the 26th of December 1881. Her birthday, only two days after mine, has always been a special date in my life because she was very special, both as a woman and as a grandmother. During recreation, I went into the courtyard with my friend Gabe Antelope from the Nez Perce tribe. At Marion, at least, I could go out into the open air and look at the deer on the other side of the barbed wire fence. I closed my eyes and imagined that I was one of those deer beyond the enclosure. I could smell the scent of the grass under the snow and the moss on the cedar bark. I also felt the warmth of the winter sun on my back. As a deer, I was alert, highly aware of any noise that could put me on guard. I didn't want to lose my companions so when they started to move, I leapt behind them. We went bounding up the hill. From the summit, I could see the prison yard and greet my friend Antelope. I wasn't sad for him. I knew that if he wanted, he too could jump over the fence. When I re-opened my eyes, I was very happy. I felt strong and rested as if I had slept for eight hours in the shade of an oak tree and I had been awakened by robins singing. I certainly couldn't complain about not having received any presents that Christmas!

    When I went back to my cell, I found another surprise waiting for me. It was a letter from Piacenza. It was signed, by Antonella Bassi and Sandra Esposito. I had never heard of them. They told me that together with some other friends, they had formed a group that corresponded with Native American prisoners and tried to obtain support and legal assistance for them. They had found out about me from some other Indian prisoners, but they didn't know the details of my story. They invited me to write it for them.

At first, I thought it was a joke. Put yourselves in my shoes. How could I believe that some people unknown to me, living in another country, wanted to help me?

I was so confused that I didn't even tell Antelope about that letter. I hid it among my papers, and left it there for more than a month. Then, one morning, suddenly, I woke from my sleep without knowing what I had dreamed, but with an urgent sense that I had to find that letter again. I read it over again, and this time I thought, "what if it's not a joke?"

I had nothing to lose. I wrote out my story, and sent it to Italy after having consulted a geographical atlas to find out where on earth Italy was. I wanted to know what route around the world those words had taken. Within very little time, I began to receive tens, then hundreds of letters. My friends had put an end for good to my days without mail. Not much longer after our correspondence started, their petitions succeeded in getting me transferred, even though governor Mickelson had sworn never to let me set foot in South Dakota again.[11]

---

[11] Governor George S. Mickelson served two terms, starting 6 January 1987. He died in a plane crash in 1993, during his second term. In 1990, the late George Mickelson, who was then the Republican Governor of South Dakota, declared that the Indian and non-Indian residents of the state should put behind their differences and try to understand each other. In an official act, the Governor even went as far as to proclaim 1990 the "Year of Reconciliation." Despite this promising statement of intent, Mickelson firmly opposed any return of Black Hills land to the Lakota. In a letter to Senator Bradley, Mickelson wrote: "It [the prospect of return of the Black Hills] continues to create false hope, which is the most cruel of things to do to people serves only to delay a final

Today I have hundreds of people writing me, especially in Europe. Support groups in my name exist in Italy, Germany, Holland, Denmark, Belgium, and England. Two different music bands, one in England and the other in Italy, have written songs about me. At times, it even seems impossible to me that I can be the central figure of this "movie". At times, I fear that it is all a dream from which, sooner or later, I will have to wake up. My pen friends, all of you, keep telling me to take it easy. It isn't a dream. But you will never succeed in convincing me that there isn't a touch of magic at work. It's enough to think that one of the two women who started all this doesn't even speak English! At times, the emotion is so powerful that it almost takes my breath away. The first time that I spoke to Sandra on the telephone, my heart was beating wildly. When I called Gloria for the first time, it was even worse. At a certain point, she had to ask if I was still there. I was there, but my voice had gone. I am almost thirty-nine years of age, and I am a warrior, but there are things that make me go back to being more bashful than a child. You have done things that have moved me in a way that I have never experienced before.

    I thought that I was the only one left who was interested in helping those who can offer nothing in return. In my tribe, this doesn't happen anymore, even if it was the

---

resolution to the entire problem . . . The Sioux people desperately need to be brought into the economic mainstream of society. Creating more divisions between the Sioux people and their fellow South Dakotans is not only wrong but a giant step backwards." By these words Mickelson made clear what he meant by "final resolution to the entire problem." In his view, Lakota people should quit complaining about the injustices they were subject to, give up wanting their sacred lands returned, take the money, and join the American Dream.

way of our chiefs. You have restored my faith in human nature. My friends belong to this unique race. It doesn't matter to me which of the colors of the Four Directions they belong. The fact that some men and women of another race and culture have chosen even to fast with me, in order to give strength to my prayers acknowledging that in our culture prayers are heard only if accompanied by a sacrifice, has made me proud. I thought, "My friends know what love is." Feeling loved and respected is important. Perhaps it is the most important thing of all. If there is love, communication knows neither borders nor limits.

I will remember for the rest of my life what took place on June 21^{st,} 1992. It was the day we Indians detained in Marion were allowed to celebrate our purification ceremony, the *inipi,* or sweat lodge. On the other side of the world, in the countryside just outside of Milan, many of my *kodas* were burning offerings of tobacco for my freedom. I could feel their presence with such intensity that I was almost overwhelmed.

When the ceremony was over, we went back into the cells and had dinner. A little later, I heard a whistle exactly like the secret whistle that I used to call King with. I was shocked. No one else knew about that distinctive whistle. When I went out for the evening recreation, I tried to find out who could have been whistling that way. On the barbed wire above the fence, I caught sight of a mockingbird. As soon as the bird saw me, it whistled. I was so excited. I tried to whistle back, and the bird replied to me. Other prisoners imitated the sound, and the mockingbird, like a well-trained violinist, replied to them as well. In the end, its whistle became an uninterrupted melody. It didn't stop even when we all went back to our cells. I sat down at the window to observe that magic bird, but he had another surprise for me. He flew onto my windowsill, came in through the bars, and sat down on my cell floor. As soon as the bird had landed, he fanned out the feathers of his tail, stretched his wings, and

BEGAN TO DANCE! Dancing, in our culture, is one of the most evocative ways of expressing feelings and recounting events. In our rituals and ceremonies, dance is an indispensable element, and we have different dances to celebrate different occasions. My brother Mike is a traditional dancer. He dances so well, in an almost divine manner. But even Mike has never managed to dance with the grace of that mockingbird in my cell! Its dance gave me a special strength. In some way, I knew that the bird was the vehicle for a personal message sent by my brothers and sisters across the seas. In his dance, I could almost hear the words: "A little longer, and something good will come."

On the 29th of December of that same year, at five in the morning, the door of my cell opened, and a guard said to me, "Get dressed and get your gear together. You're being transferred. You are going to Sioux Falls."

A little more than a year had passed since the arrival of the letter from Sandra and Antonella. In one year and three days, my Italian friends had achieved something that judges had refused to do, despite the fact that it was what the law dictated. The twenty-two months of my federal sentence had elapsed some time previously, but without the international campaign in my support, I would have been left to rot within the walls of Marion, where I didn't even have access to the legal papers pertaining to my case, since the South Dakota State had neglected to send them to me there.

Without your help, I would probably be dead by now—maybe from the lack of medical treatment, which they were withholding when the pain from the concussion caused by the accident during my transfer was driving me mad; or otherwise at the hands of one of their hired assassins, allowed to act in the darkness and with impunity when no one was around to watch. Instead, my jailers have now realized that every one of their moves is under scrutiny – studied, made public, discussed and criticized by an army of people all over the world. They are running scared. They are afraid of journalists like Gloria, who might expose their actions to the public opinion. They cannot understand how it could have happened that there are famous lawyers that have now come to my assistance, from Italy and England. And they are concerned about the avalanche of faxes and letters of protest that they received regarding how poorly they have treated me. Their hatred has grown because of their anger at seeing that I am no longer alone. But their fear is also growing. They don't dare to attack me as they would have done before. And like I said, should they still try to do me in, they wouldn't have the courage to act arrogantly. They shiver in fear like jackrabbits. Even wrapped up as they are under the protection of their guns and laws and uniforms, they can feel your power.

When Dr. Vincent Di Maio sent me the copy of his findings – seventy-seven words, containing the key to my freedom – they got nervous. Perhaps they thought, if in just five months of investigation, this Italian journalist has managed to get this far, will the day also come when that Indian bastard succeeds in getting a new trial?

There is no doubt that I'll do it. That bastard himself is telling you so. This bastard, who no longer has to fight alone. That day is not far off. And that day…

I imagine that day. I dream about it every night. That day, I will give you all back what you've given me. At least, I will try. It might take me a while, though. There are not enough hours in a single day for that.

The Black Hills are not for sale

By Daniele Bolelli

Sylvan Lake, in the Black Hills

The Black Hills of South Dakota represent many things to many people. To the Lakota people, they are *Wamaka Og'naka Icante*, "the heart of everything that is", the spiritual center of the universe, the place where the

Lakota Nation was born after emerging from the ground. To many Indian tribes the Black Hills were a treasure offering abundant game in times of need, medicinal plants, tipi poles and protection from the freezing prairie winter. To many Euro-Americans, they were a promised land where gold could be found in the streams and in the grass. Today, they are the site of the national monument of Mount Rushmore and a thriving tourist industry. Because of the Black Hills, George Armstrong Custer was admitted to the Paradise of The Most Celebrated Losers of All Times. Wild Bill Hickok, Calamity Jane, and a whole pantheon of Wild West heroes and villains turned them into their temporary home. Former basketball star and former presidential candidate Bill Bradley introduced a proposal to Congress to return them to the Lakota people. For their sake, the poorest people in the United States still refuse to accept over 500 million dollars. For their sake, the Lakota people and the United States went to war, and to this very day they are still engaged in the longest legal battle in the nation's history. The Black Hills are definitely much more than simple mountains. They are a source of dreams, power, wealth, ethnic identity and conflict between nations.

In 1887, while building his home near modern day Spearfish, in the northern part of the Black Hills, a certain Louis Thoen found himself face to face with a haunting message. On a flat piece of limestone he had just unearthed was scratched a message that sent shivers down his spine. It read:

"Came to the Hills in 1833 seven of us DeLacompt, Ezra Kind, G. W. Wood,
    T. Brown, R. Kent, Wm. King, Indian Crow. All died but me Ezra Kind.
    Killed by Ind. beyond the high hill got our gold in 1834. Got all the gold

we could carry our ponys got by Indians I have lost my gun and nothing to eat and Indians hunting me."

Ezra Kind—whomever he might have been—never made it back to tell his story. His remains likely still rest in the Black Hills and his scalp probably ended up adorning the lodge of some Lakota or Cheyenne warrior. Besides being powerfully eerie, his last attempt to communicate with the outside world tells us that the tribes didn't take kindly to foreigners coming into the Black Hills.

Less than a couple of decades after Ezra Kind's unfortunate trip, a gold-seeking party discovered the same truth the hard way. In 1852, thirty men attempted to reach the Hills. Eight changed their minds after spotting Indians watching them, the other twenty-two were never heard from again. As these examples make abundantly clear, the Lakota were more than a bit sensitive about any intrusion in the Black Hills. What they feared most was that Euro-Americans would learn that the Hills were rich in "the yellow stone that made white men crazy". This is why they kept outsiders at bay. And this is also why in a special tribal council held in 1857 in the Black Hills, the Lakota decided to kill any tribal member guilty of revealing the presence of gold to non-Indians. If this secret was discovered—they rightfully predicted—they would have an invasion on their hands.

Why were the Lakota so concerned about the Black Hills? Because the Paha Sapa—their term for "black mountains"—were not just like any other piece of their homeland. Everything about the Black Hills screamed that they were a special place. Located in the mostly flat lands of the western portion of South Dakota, they rose up, seemingly out of nowhere. Because of the contrast between their high peaks and the surrounding flat lands, on a clear day they could be seen from many miles away, in any direction. In countless ways, the Black Hills were and still are everything that the rest of the area is not. They are temperate in winter and offer protection from the blizzards that sweep the prairies. They are dotted with lakes and covered with beautiful cedars and ponderosa pines that give shelter against the summer heat. They are a dream come true for any hunting peoples since they are home to many species of animals. They truly look like a little heaven on earth. And the Lakota and Cheyenne valued them for more than their spectacular physical characteristics. The Cheyenne cultural hero, Sweet Medicine, received the teachings that have shaped the Cheyenne society at Bear Butte, one of the main peaks at the outskirts of the Black Hills. The vision of Black Elk, the famous Lakota holy man whose life was immortalized in the classic Black Elk Speaks, took place in the Black Hills. And in one version of their creation story, the Lakota tell that they used to live underneath the ground until they emerged on this earth through a hole in a rock located in the Wind Cave, in the southern portion of the Hills.

The Black Hills, in other words, are sacred lands; they are *wakan*—charged with a sacred power unlike what can be found anywhere else.

Western historians push a considerably less romantic vision of the Lakota connection to the Hills, since many of them argue that the Lakota first arrived in the area in 1775 during a westward migration and pushed other tribes out by force. But the Lakota dismiss this as a thinly veiled effort to justify the later conquest by the United States.

The U.S. government first became interested in the area of the Great Plains after convincing in 1803 the representatives of a cash-strapped Napoleon to sign away title to lands that they weren't controlling anyway. With what became known as the Louisiana Purchase, the American government bought from the French nominal ownership to most of the Midwest—which is ironic, considering that the Midwest was in the hands of tribes that had barely heard of either the Americans or the French. None of this mattered to the Americans or to any European powers, since they didn't recognize the right of "savages" to own land. But despite being drunk on racism, they were not so self-deluded as to think that the tribes would simply move aside once they showed them a piece of paper. They knew they would have to fight for it, but were in no hurry to do it. During the first half of the 1800s, Americans mostly left the Lakota and their lands alone (with the exception of a few guys like good, old Ezra Kind). Most American settlers simply wanted to travel through Lakota lands on their way to California and other western destinations. To ensure that they could do so without finding themselves on the receiving hand of an arrow through the skull, in 1851 the U.S. government invited the Lakota, along with other tribes, to sign the first Fort Laramie Treaty: the tribes would agree to let American settlers pass unmolested, and in exchange the United States would pay them in goods for their trouble. In one of the provisions of the treaty, the U.S. government acknowledged that the Black Hills region (and much more) was in full possession of the Lakota.

This exchange of pleasantries didn't last. Eventually, the increasing number of wagons coming from the East began disrupting the bison migrations. And unhappy bison quickly translated into unhappy Lakota. Open hostilities between the Lakota and their Cheyenne allies on one side and the United States on the other began in 1854, when Lieutenant Grattan failed Diplomacy 101 in ordering his men to open fire on a Lakota leader during some tense negotiations. Enraged, other Lakota proceeded to wipe out

Grattan and his men. This was the opening bell signaling the beginning of over twenty years of intermittent warfare.

For over two decades, the Lakota offered a master class in guerrilla tactics. Being nomadic buffalo-hunters, riders and warriors since childhood, the Lakota proved difficult to track down and equally difficult to defeat. After more than a decade of fruitless fighting, the government agreed to cease the conflict and sign a treaty (the 1868 Fort Laramie Treaty) that was very favorable to the tribes: big chunks of the Dakotas (including the Black Hills) would be theirs "as long as the grass shall grow and the rivers shall flow", and—more importantly—75% of the tribe would have to agree to any future sale of land. This was music to the Lakota ears. What the sweet music of the Treaty was covering up, though, was the sound of the guns of professional buffalo hunters wiping out the bison herds at a steady pace. The U.S. government understood that it was only a matter of time until the Lakota economy would be destroyed making the tribe much more vulnerable to conquest. The once 40 million bison populating the Plains were now down to a few thousands and still shrinking.

And yet the bison stampede on the road to extinction wasn't happening quickly enough for some people. In 1874, just six years after the signing of the treaty, a military expedition under the command of Lieutenant Colonel George Armstrong Custer went into the Black Hills. The point of the expedition was to verify rumors that gold deposits existed in the Hills—precisely what the Lakota feared most. If confirmed, this news would send thousands of squatters packing for the Hills, would force the Lakota to retaliate and in turn would force the government to precipitate a war with the tribes. Among those hoping for this result were the good folks from the Northern Pacific Railroad: for years they had tried to carve their way through Indian lands, and they had been recently stopped east of the Missouri River by the economic crisis of 1873. But a gold rush in the Black Hills would stimulate white settlement, remove the Indian obstacle and attract investors who would boost the finances of the troubled company. Custer would be their Jesus resurrecting the Railroad from the dead.

And Custer delivered just as he had promised. The second he returned from the Black Hills with tales of gold to be found everywhere, the titles of the newspaper Yankton Press & Dakotaian euphemistically announced "Prepare for Lively Times". Lively times indeed as a horde of squatters hungry for gold flooded into the Black Hills in violation of the Fort Laramie Treaty. After a couple half-hearted attempts to stop them, the government threw in the towel on that effort and turned instead to the Lakota trying to convince them to sell the land. Some Lakota leaders such as Red Cloud were willing to have this discussion. Others such as Sitting Bull and Crazy Horse let it be known in no uncertain terms what they thought of selling Lakota sacred lands to the Americans. Neither one of them bothered to show up at the negotiations, but just to make sure that this could be misunderstood as disinterest Crazy Horse sent three hundred warriors to deliver his message. As a few Lakota leaders and government negotiators were haggling over price, Crazy Horse warriors arrived riding into camp and—guns in hand—singing, "The Black Hills are my land and I love it. And whoever interferes will hear this gun."

And with that, negotiations were over.

Unable to gather the necessary number of signatures required by the 1868 Fort Laramie Treaty, the government decided to dispense with legal technicalities. They were going to get the Hills one way or another. As the Bismark Tribune stated, "The American people need the country the

Indians now occupy; many of our people are out of employment; the masses need some new excitement . . . An Indian war would do no harm, for it must come, sooner, or later." Expressing a similar idea, Lieutenant Colonel Richard Irving Dodge wrote to General Crook: "None but a ring ridden [meek] nation would ever think for one moment of leaving such paradise in the hands of miserable savages." In this climate, President Grant decided that the Fort Laramie Treaty was good for toilet paper. Grant, after all, had already stated that the interests of the settlers were to be protected "even if the extermination of every Indian tribe was necessary to secure such a result." Such genocidal fantasies were shared by other elite members of the military. General William Sherman in a letter to Grant had written: "We must act with vindictive earnestness against the Sioux, even to their extermination, men, women and children. Nothing less will reach the root of the case." The popular press echoed these sentiments. The Kansas Daily Tribune argued: "There can be no permanent, lasting peace on the frontier till these devils are exterminated." The Board of Health of a Black Hills town took this advice to heart when it commended a man who had brought Indian scalps because they argued that murdering Indians was beneficial to the health of the settlement. The paradox of admitting that the law was on the Indian side while dreaming of their extermination did not seem to trouble too many people in the 1870s. The pages of the Chicago Inter-Ocean thundered: "What, to the roaming Yankee, are the links that bind the red man to the home of his fathers? He is but an episode in the advance of the Caucasian. He must decrease that the new comers may grow in wealth." And Annie Tallent, the only female member of the first group of gold-seekers to reach the Black Hills, mused: "Ignoring the ethical side of the question, should such treaties as tend to arrest the advance of civilization, and retard the development of the rich resources of our country, ever have been entered into?"

Tallent didn't need to worry. During this phase of its history, the government would prove itself very adept at "ignoring the ethical side of the question". The ideology of Manifest Destiny was alive and strong, prodding the nation toward war against any tribe standing in the way of American expansion. The outcome of the war was already written: a nation of millions against tribes numbering a few thousands... and yet Lakota and Cheyenne would not just go away without a fight. On June 25, 1876, George Armstrong Custer, the man who had discovered gold in the Black Hills and helped precipitate the war, rushed to attack an Indian camp on the Little Big Horn hoping to cash in on some glory before the war would end.

Bad idea.

Just as the nation was close to celebrating the 100 year anniversary of The Declaration of Independence, the Lakota and Cheyenne beat back the U.S. Army attack, killing Custer along with hundreds of his troops.

The victory, however, was short-lived. The buffalo herds were indeed almost completely destroyed and within a year all the Lakota and Cheyenne in the United States had to surrender due to lack of food. Just to make sure that the Lakota would not think of rebelling, the army set up a political assassination as Crazy Horse's reward for surrendering. A similar destiny awaited the other pillar of Lakota resistance, Sitting Bull, when he returned from his exile in Canada a few years later. Government policy toward Lakota leadership seemed to have stolen a page from Michael Corleone's playbook. As all of this was happening, the government made another attempt to acquire title to the Black Hills. Despite threatening Indians with starvation and possible violence, the 1877 Manypenny Commission managed to gather the signatures of less than 10% of the Lakota adult males, far short of the 75% required by the law. However, demonstrating that math is an opinion, Congress ratified the document and created the illusion that the U.S. government had "legally" acquired the Black Hills. Despite these feeble attempts at saving face, it is safe to assume that probably hardly anyone in the United States was too disturbed by the government's illegal actions. Writing a few years after these facts, Theodore Roosevelt makes this clear, "Whether the whites won the land by treaty, by armed conquest, or, as was actually the case, by a mixture of both, mattered comparatively little so long as the land was won. It was all-important that it should be won for the benefit of civilization and in the interests of mankind."

Isn't that great? 'Stealing land' has an ugly ring to it. 'Advancing the interests of mankind' sounds so much better.

In the aftermath of all this, the Lakota took a beating. The subsequent decades of Lakota history were made of forced assimilation, the Wounded Knee massacre, no economic prospects, boarding schools where kids would be beaten for speaking their tribal language, their religious ceremonies being outlawed (so much for the idea of freedom of religion in the United States)… But despite all this, the tribe didn't forget about the Black Hills, and in the 1920s they hired lawyers to address the blatant violation of the Fort Laramie Treaty. A string of losses in court lasting almost thirty years didn't dampen their determination to pursue the case. Not that they had many illusions regarding their chances. After all, they were fighting for a case in which the U.S. government was the defendant as well as judge and jury. There was not much of a logical basis to hope that the courts would side with the Indians. But had the Lakota being logical, they should have given up hope (about this case and everything else in their lives) decades earlier. It did not matter how bad the odds looked. They were the only odds they had.

A change of lawyers in the 1950s gave them a second chance. And almost a quarter of century later, after an interminable list of appeals and counter-appeals, the Black Hills claim had its day in front of the highest court in the land. In 1980, the U.S. Supreme Court confirmed what the Lakota had argued all along: the Black Hills had been taken illegally. In the words of one of the justices, there had never been in the nation's history "a more ripe and rank case of dishonorable dealings" than the way the government had obtained the Black Hills.

And yet...

In one of the strangest moments in this century-old battle, the Lakota didn't accept their victory. When the Supreme Court awarded the tribe several millions of dollars as compensation for the theft of the Black Hills, the Lakota refused the cash.

That's right, a tribe living in some of the very poorest counties in the United States turned down the payment.

Had the Supreme Court ruling happened decades earlier, when Lakota hopes for the future were painfully low, this judgment would have possibly put an end to this battle. But like a carefully scripted drama, a major twist was about to take place in this story. By 1980, the cultural climate on most Lakota reservations had changed profoundly. After decades in which boarding schools, missionaries, and government policies did their best to instill a sense of shame of being Indian, the 1960s and 1970s saw a resurgence of Indian pride. By 1980, accepting monetary compensation was no longer an honorable option. What most Lakota wanted was not money, but the Black Hills themselves.

"The Black Hills Are Not For Sale" had become the Lakota battle cry on most reservations. Accepting the money would be equivalent to selling out one's sacred lands.

So, through the efforts of Lakota attorney Mario Gonzales, they rejected the money preferring instead to push for a return of the land. In this effort, the Lakota found a champion in Bill Bradley, the former basketball star and U.S. Senator from New Jersey, who would introduce a bill to Congress regarding the return of the Black Hills. The bill was clearly a compromise: the Lakota wouldn't ask for everything that was stolen, but only of all the federally held land in the Black Hills (1.3 million acres). Mount Rushmore would remain in the government's hands and private property would be untouched.

Had Bradley proposed to burn down the White House and feed babies to hungry mountain lions, he may have encountered a warmer reception in South Dakota. The state congressional delegation (including some of Bradley's fellow Democrats) had a fit, and their reaction effectively killed any chance of the bill passing. Bradley introduced the Bill again in 1987. Phil Stevens, a Californian millionaire claiming to be the great-grandson of Henry Standing Bear, had managed to convince Mario Gonzales, Oliver Red Cloud and his supporters on Pine Ridge Reservation that he was the right man to obtain the return of their lands. Stevens then had his local congressman introduce his own version of a bill to return the Black Hills to the Lakota plus an additional amount of monetary damages—a bill that everyone but Stevens and his supporters considered impossibly unrealistic. Despite Stevens' promises, the Martinez Bill, as it was called, did not achieve any meaningful result other than giving ammunition to the opponents of any land return to argue that Lakota factionalism prevented any solution that would please the whole tribe.

Ask the U.S. government, and they'll tell you the Black Hills issue has been resolved. Ask the Lakota people, and you'll get a very different answer.

Ever since the end of the 1980s, the Black Hills Claim has been laying dormant, yet not dead. No discernible strategy showing some potential to succeed is in sight. But this does not mean that after almost 150 years, the Lakota have given up hope to get the Black Hills back. The money they were awarded by the Supreme Court in 1980 has been sitting in a bank accumulating interests, and yet despite the fact that they live in the poorest counties of one of the most materialistic nations on earth the Lakota continue to refuse to touch it. Lakota pride and identity today are tied to the Black Hills just as much as they were in the 1870s. Is it unrealistic for the Lakota to hope to get the Black Hills back? Of course it is. It was also unrealistic for Jewish people to imagine they could get Israel back after almost 2000 years, but it happened anyway. Had they given up hope and been "realistic," their return to Israel would have never taken place. And for many Lakota today, the Black Hills are no less significant than Israel is for Jews. The battle for the Black Hills is not one that is about to end anytime soon.

Other Black Hills Stories

Yellow Thunder Camp

In 1981, with their legal options to get back the Black Hills dwindling, some members of AIM decided to take matters in their own hands. As AIM member Bill Means (the brother of Russell) declared, "If Indian people think we can get the Black Hills back only by going to Court, then we must not remember our history." On the appointed day, twenty cars containing little over fifty AIM members left the Pine Ridge reservation and headed for Victoria Creek Canyon, a beautiful location in the Black Hills, about twelve miles from Rapid City, which was surrounded by ponderosa pines, had a pond and good running water. Their goal was to set up an alternative-energy community, and a live-in school for Indian children. The Lakota brought with them materials for erecting teepees, geodesic domes, and sweat lodges, and began to set up camp on federal land. Their camp was named in honor of Raymond Yellow Thunder, a Lakota man who had been killed in 1972 in Nebraska by local racists who were never convicted. His case had become symbolic of the injustices still plaguing Native Peoples in those days. The legal basis for the occupation was the undisturbed use of the Black Hills guaranteed to the Lakota by the 1868 Fort Laramie Treaty, and the American Indian Freedom of Religion Act of 1978, and an 1897 legislation permitting communities to use National Forests for establishing schools and churches. In an attempt to follow the letter of the law, Lakota spiritual leader Matthew King filed a claim with the U.S. Forest Service for 800 acres of surrounding forest to be granted to establish a school and a spiritual camp. In a less diplomatic move, Russell Means challenged his long-time nemesis Governor William Janklow to a fistfight for the right to stay on the land. If Means lost, AIM member would leave. Otherwise, they would stay unmolested. Needless to say, Janklow wasn't amused with Means' creative solution and turned him down.

While waiting for the Forest Service's answer, members of the Yellow Thunder camp began to make the place their home. The ninety-three year old spiritual leader

Frank Fools Crow came to bless the camp. Children began to attend the school where they took, among other subjects, courses in Lakota language. Subsistence activities included raising goats and chickens, as well as fishing in the creek and planting a garden for vegetables. The camp's showers, water heater, oven, and dryer all run on solar energy.
Representatives from all the Lakota reservations came to visit the camp and show their support.

Things, however, were not running smoothly on the legal front. James Mathers, the Forest Service Supervisor in charge of the case, denied their application. "I have based my decision upon an evaluation of several alternatives—wrote Mathers—and have determined that your proposed community development is not in the public interest." Somehow it appears that any project that involved American Indians was not—in the eyes of the Forest Service—"in the public interest." Over the previous five and half years, in fact, the Forest Service had granted fifty-eight permits for projects similar to the one proposed by the Yellow Thunder Camp, and denied only four. Three out of those four had been filed by Indian people.

Despite this setback, AIM kept fighting this decision in appeal after appeal, while its members went on living in the Black Hills—the first time in over a hundred years that a Lakota camp functioned year around within their sacred lands. Camp members found themselves occasionally harassed by local rednecks, but these were more like cases of posturing than legitimate threats. Real violence, however, erupted when an undercover informant working for the U.S. Marshal's Service got into a fight with and killed a local man who had decided to use Yellow Thunder camp for target shooting. The FBI promptly jumped on this to request that a judge orders immediate closure of the camp but the judge refused since the violence had been instigated by an agent provocateur. And yet legal victories would end right there. After the last appeal was done, and Yellow Thunder residents had run out of options to legally claim the land, they decided to fold. It had been a glorious experiment, but it had run its course.

In many ways, the government's refusal to grant to the Yellow Thunder Camp legal permission to exist seems ironic. The Yellow Thunder Camp offered the option of creating a community that would benefit the vast Lakota population of the state, and would serve as a working model for a place that worked on renewable energy. What the Forest Service proposed for the same area of land was to log the place, and build gravel pits. This—according to the Forest Service—would better serve the needs of the community. Furthermore, the government supported the environmentally destructive practices of energy companies that were planning to turn the Black Hills into a national sacrifice area.

For the Lakota, it was a brief but meaningful example of how an environmentally sensitive community offering a meaningful alternative to the bleak conditions on the reservations can be created. Through their own sheer determination, with great initiative and imagination, some Lakota had stopped waiting for the government to solve their problems and had taken charge of their destiny by building the kind of community that they wanted to live in. For many of the people who lived there, whether for a few weeks or years, it was a life-altering experience that left them with a sense of possibility unparalleled by anything they normally experienced on the reservation. Its ultimate demise in the face of overwhelming legal obstacles did not cancel the fact that for a period of time the community breathed life of its own. For a while, the idea at the roots of Yellow Thunder Camp proved that it could work. And if the dream of a community based on a better view of the place of human beings on earth could work at some point, it means that it can work again.

From Dunbar to Tatanka

One more round in the war for the Black Hills. The most recent episode of this saga is the story of an old man who, for the sake of the Black Hills, went to battle against one of the biggest movie stars of the 1990s. To support him in his corner, the movie star had his international fame, the State of South Dakota, the Forest Service, and powerful financial investors. In his corner, the old man had extreme poverty, weak health, and three-quarters of a century of a hard life hanging on his shoulders. A fair fight? Not even close. The old man also had in his corner a wicked sense of humor, the devotion of hundreds of Lakota who considered him a spiritual leader, and the fact that he dreamed of the Thunder Beings, some of the most powerful spirits in the Lakota pantheon. Unfortunately, he was the only one who believed that these last three factors could make a difference. If this were a prize fight, the bookies would not have even accepted bets. But the old man was not one to care about unfavorable odds. After all, he came from a people whose battle-cry was "Hoka Hey" (loosely translated as "Today Is a Good Day to Die.") If difficulties could stop him, he would have stopped long ago. Fighting against overwhelming odds was not going to intimidate him. And so the old man put on his characteristic cowboy hat, opened the door, and walked out ready for the fight. Let's go to battle, old man. "Hoka Hey."

In 1990, American Indian peoples in general, and the Lakota people in specific, found themselves in the Hollywood spotlights. This, in fact, was the time when the movie *Dances with Wolves* was released worldwide and became an instant success. The creation of actor/director

Kevin Costner, *Dances with Wolves* was filmed in South Dakota, in the hearth of Lakota country. It told the story of an American soldier who in the 1860s abandons his post to go reside among the Lakota. Adopted by the tribe, he lives as one of them fighting against their Indian enemies, participating in their buffalo hunts, and trying to oppose American intrusion into their lands. *Dances with Wolves* easily turned out to be the movie of the year, ending up winning seven Academy Awards, including one for Best Picture, and earning more than $500 million (from a $18 million investment). Many Lakota liked *Dances with Wolves* very much. Costner had hired almost 200 Indians to play the Lakota characters, and as consultants to ensure accuracy in everything from clothing styles to *teepee*-making. Even more important in the eyes of Lakota traditionalists, not only were the Lakota characters portrayed very favorably, but they spoke their own language throughout the entire movie. Non-Lakota speaking audiences got a taste of the tribal language and had to read English subtitles for a good part of the movie.

For a brief period, anything having to do with Indian culture became fashionable. College courses about the history and culture of American Indian peoples were in high demand, books on the same topic enjoyed some mainstream attention, and more movies about Indians were released. While good feelings between Costner and the Lakota still prevailed, Costner was adopted into one Lakota family during a *Hunka* ceremony—a ritual by which people created a kinship relationship with individuals they are not related to by blood.

Good feelings, however, were not destined to last. Problems began when Kevin Costner and his brother Dan decided to invest their money to create a business opportunity in the Black Hills. Already in 1990 they had bought a building in Deadwood, South Dakota, a tiny town with a colorful past located in the northern part of the Black Hills. Two years later they bought an additional eighty-five acres in the area. No problems so far. The real trouble started when in 1995 the Costner brothers bought almost 600 acres of land in Spearfish Canyon, and tried to convince the Forest Service to swap 635 acres of federally owned land near Deadwood for their private property in Spearfish.

Anyone possessing even only a passing familiarity with the Lakota efforts to regain the Black Hills could predict what their reaction to this proposed land transfer would be. Whereas they had not faulted the Costner brothers for buying private land in the Black Hills, since private land was not what they hoped to get back from Congress, acquiring federally held land was a whole different story. Federally held lands, in fact, were the ones that the Lakota had been fighting to get back. It is in the hope of regaining these lands that the poorest people in the United States still refused almost 600 million in compensation. If any Black Hills land had a possibility of being returned, this was it. Trading private property for federal land meant making sure that more Black Hills acres would never be returned to the Lakota people.

To add insult to injury, the purpose for which the Costner brothers wanted this land further infuriated the Lakota. The "Dunbar" Project, as it was called after the last name of the character played by Kevin Costner in *Dances with Wolves*, consisted in building a five star hotel, a casino, and a giant golf course just outside of Deadwood. In a state in which gambling is one of the very few sources of revenue that the tribes control, building a giant casino next to Mount Rushmore and the Rapid City airport was a sure way to take preciously needed money away from the reservation communities. After a 1987 fire had destroyed much of

Deadwood's main street, in an effort to revitalize the local economy, the state had legalized gambling in this town; the only place in South Dakota with legal gambling other than Indian reservations. Nothing of the scale proposed by the Costner brothers, however, existed in town. The gambling competition, however, was not what worried the Lakota. Costner had hinted that he wanted to build a casino on his own private property in Deadwood since 1992 and no one had complained. But taking federally owned land to build a giant money-making entertainment playground for rich non-Indian tourists was not something the Lakota could take very well. If this was not enough, Costner was also planning to acquire title to enough land to build a railway system that would cut through the Black Hills and connect the Dunbar to the Rapid City airport, forty-two miles away.

Most Lakota were disgusted with the idea, and felt betrayed by yet another Euro-American who had come among them as a friend but seemed ready to take advantage of them. Those Lakota who were still willing to give Costner a chance quickly changed their minds after hearing the Costners' response to their concerns. Terry Krantz, the Costners' right hand man for this project, declared that *Dances with Wolves* was only a movie and that Kevin Costner was in no way morally obliged to Indian peoples because he had made money from the film. Continuing the public relations disaster, Krantz added that it was unfair to expect Costner to suffer economically only because he was a friend of the Indians.

At this point of the story, enters Sidney Keith. In fact, if the Lakota attachment to the Black Hills were not as much part of who they are as their own flesh and blood, this would have been the end. The state of South Dakota wanted to see this project completed and was ready to back it up at all costs. The Costner brothers had the right connections to invest in this project more money than almost all members of the Lakota nation put together made in a year. But the Lakota are still too attached to the Black Hills not to fight for them. Giving up was not an option. One of the main figures to lead the Lakota against the Dunbar project was—in 1995—a seventy-five year old man with his ever present dark shades and cowboy hat, Sidney Keith. Born on the Cheyenne River reservation, in the northern part of South Dakota, on October 15, 1919, Keith eventually became a spiritual leader for many Lakota. Under the guidance of revered Lakota holy men Frank Fools Crow and Matthew King, Keith spearheaded the movement for the return of the traditional Sun Dance ceremony on Cheyenne River. Throughout his life, Keith worked incessantly to keep the Lakota culture alive. He was one of the Indian advisors who helped with the creation of the Journey Museum in Rapid City. He authored a Lakota-English dictionary. He helped hundreds of Indians rediscover their tribal idiom by teaching Lakota language classes at the Oglala Lakota College, one of the most important community colleges in the nation run by an Indian tribe.

    The image that defines Keith in my mind comes from a 1995 Sun Dance that I attended with my mother, as invited guests. Although Sidney had led the ceremony since 1970, he had never put himself through the highest test of the ritual: the sacrifice made by the dancers who shed their blood as a prayer for the benefit of all. When he announced his intention to pierce during that year's Sun Dance, many people questioned whether he could make it out alive. When the time came, seeing an old man who walked with the help of a cane and was affected by arthritis and diabetes go through such an extreme physical trial brought tears to the eyes of many supporters. But proving all catastrophic predictions wrong, Keith was back to telling jokes within minutes after the end of the ceremony. If the Lakota needed a tough fighter to help them stop the Dunbar project, Keith was definitely a good candidate.

It was just a few months before this Sun Dance that the controversy over the Dunbar project exploded. When the Lakota community got wind of the Costner brothers' intention to swap their land in Spearfish Canyon for the Forest Service land near Deadwood, Keith emerged as one of the leaders of the Indian opposition to the Dunbar (immediately renamed "The Dumb Bear" by Keith.) On May 20, 1995, Keith organized a protest march that traveled from Bear Butte, which rises just outside the town of Sturgis, to the location of the proposed land swap in Deadwood. When the protesters reached their destination, a drum group from the Cheyenne River Reservation began a series of songs about the significance of the Black Hills. Keith then prayed in Lakota for the welfare of the land. Somehow what was going on in this little corner of South Dakota managed to make international news. The picture of Keith praying, surrounded by the pines of the Black Hills, in front of a ceremonial staff with twelve eagle feathers attached to it while his wife Shirley and other protesters stood in the background, was published around the globe.

Keith was quoted in the London Times as saying; "He [Costner] used Indians . . . He didn't try to help the people. He is greedy." Among the Lakota, who hold generosity to be one of their four cardinal virtues, being accused of greediness is serious business. A Lakota protester added: "I thought he understood what we're up against as Indian people. I'd have to be foolish to try and put a casino on top of a church. To us, the Black Hills are sacred. They are a church to us." And Mitchell Zephier, another Lakota opponent of the Dunbar, stated: "It comes down to whether or not we hold the earth to be sacred."

Despite an outpour of Lakota voices speaking against the land swap, the Forest Service ended up accepting the Costners' proposal—an event which planted a legacy of distrust that made many Lakota skeptical for years to come of the Forest Service stated efforts to become more sensitive to the needs of the Indian people of South Dakota. Despite this defeat, Keith did not lose his sense of humor and often joked about the major financial disaster of Costner's movie Waterworld as karmic payback for what the actor was doing in the Black Hills.

The few books that discuss the conflict over the Dunbar end the story here: Kevin Costner comes across as another Euro-American betraying the Indians' trust, the government as always favoring profit over Indian rights, and the Lakota as perennial losers of yet another morally valid but unsuccessful battle. But further developments prove this picture wrong. In fact, even in the face of the setback suffered with the Forest Service's decision, in the years to come the Lakota continued their opposition to the project, and wrote over 13,000 letters to the Costner brothers. This massive mailing led to Kevin Costner deciding to meet with Arvol Looking Horse, a Lakota religious leader who is the Keeper of the Buffalo Calf Pipe, which according to tradition had been given to the Lakota at the dawn of time by the cultural heroine White Buffalo Calf Woman. During the meeting, Looking Horse explained yet another time about the importance of the Black Hills for the Lakota. Costner replied that he had read the many letters that had been sent his way and was sorry for the controversy the Dunbar project had created. Furthermore, he promised he would not build the casino, luxury hotel and golf course as previously announced, but rather would create a place where people could come to learn about the Lakota culture.

No one is exactly sure about what led to this dramatic change of heart. With more than a note of cynicism, some suggest that Costner had more difficulties than expected in finding some financial backers for the Dunbar since the projected costs quickly skyrocketed far beyond the initial estimate. Others—James among them—suggest that Costner had been a good guy all along, who for a while listened to the wrong people, but who ultimately came to his senses and listened to his conscience. This decision proved emotionally costly for Costner. His brother Dan, in fact, did not take it very well, and grew so infuriated that Kevin Costner ended up requesting a restraining order to be placed against him.

Cyndi, James' wife, Kevin Costner and James, in 2009

What emerged in place of the Dunbar is "Tatanka: The Story of the Bison", a cultural and historical center focusing on Plains Indian culture in general and on the buffalo in particular. In the words of David Melmer, a correspondent for the weekly magazine *Indian Country Today*, who followed the Costner controversy from its beginning; "Tatanka: Story of the Bison is nearly a complete turnaround from what the Dunbar resort was to become ... What has emerged is not a substitute, but a better use of the land; to tell the story of the Lakota and Plains Indians through the bison."

Tatanka, (a Lakota word for buffalo,) which had its grand opening during June 2003, is an educational center featuring at its entrance fourteen larger than life bronze sculptures of buffalos being chased by three equally monumental sculpted Indian riders. Located on eighty-five acres of land, this $5 million project also features the works in progress of several artists, an interpretative exhibit about the bison, and indoor and outdoor dining. But the centerpiece of the center is the recreation of a Lakota village the way it would have looked in the 1840s. Within the village, modern day Lakota people wearing the clothes of their ancestors carry out some of the daily life activities that were characteristic of that time period. In an effort to provide an accurate historical picture, they would only speak Lakota while an interpreter standing to the side would help visitors understand the significance of what they are witnessing. Overall, 85% of the *Tatanka* fairly well paid staff is formed by American Indians. Furthermore, the center works in partnership with the Black Hills State University to offer classes in Lakota language and environmental studies. Lakota storytelling featuring elders like Albert White Hat also takes place on the site.

In his inaugural speech, Costner made clear that the two main goals of the center are to educate people about Lakota culture and environmental issues. In a tribute to the Lakota commitment to keep their culture despite decades of legal persecution, Costner said:

"So today I see this place as the beginning. A day to celebrate. To celebrate the courage it took for our brothers and sisters to hold out against a government that could not and would not protect them. We admire your courage in holding to your own language, your traditions, your spiritualism. We are finally inspired and in awe that in the face of all that we have thrown at you, that you are still standing."

It is perhaps ironic that it was precisely this Lakota "courage to hold on to your traditions" that had pit tribal members against Costner in the first place, and that made the transformation of the Dunbar into *Tatanka* possible. But still good that it happened.

Less than two months after the opening of *Tatanka*, on August 11, 2003, Kevin Costner was honored with his star on the Hollywood Walk of Fame. Perhaps Lakota jokes contained some truth, after all. If the disaster of Waterworld had been the actor's punishment for the Dunbar project, this was his reward for committing to the more sensible *Tatanka* center.

Sidney Keith never lived to see the victory of the battle that he had started. He died on June 14, 1997, of complications from pneumonia and gallstones. He was seventy-seven year old, less than two months away from leading yet another Sun Dance.
But the Sun Dance that he started in 1970 continues in the hands of the people he trained as well as his children and grandchildren. Generations of students and colleagues at the Oglala Lakota College remember him as an inspiration. And certainly, his leadership in the successful opposition against the Dunbar project is a fitting icing on the cake of a life spent trying to keep the Lakota culture alive.

If it is true that the fight against the Dunbar was a personal triumph for Keith, it is also true that it was an important victory for the Lakota in general. If anyone needs proof of the tremendous contemporary importance of the Black Hills to the Lakota people, one needs to look no further than this story. Several years of Lakota activism led to the stopping of a $500 million project that was backed by the state of South Dakota. In the place of this destructive project, the Lakota managed to help create a center that will educate people about their tribal culture and about the beauty of the Black Hills. The day of occupations in the Black Hills may be over. The court case has been over since 1980. The congressional efforts to regain land in the Black Hills are stalled and there isn't any progress or positive change in this regard. But the Dunbar-*Tatanka* story proves that the fight for the Black Hills is still going on, and that modest but significant victories can be won.

AFTERWORD

The road I rode with Jim has been a wild one. I can't even put into words everything that it has brought to my life. When we met the first time, he told me: "I never lost a battle". "Neither did I", I echoed. He laughed, and we convened that we were a good team. We both knew, though, that the battle we were facing was like no other. It had been fought and lost before. So, it required a total change of strategy, new blood, uncanny imagination, faith, a little bit of craziness and relentless willpower. Did we have it in us? You bet we did.

It still took ten years to win it—years constelled by refusals and delays, when it was hard to keep our spirits up and emotions and frustrations at bay; years filled by impossible "missions", often envisioned by Jim sitting in a cell and acted upon by me, driving all over South Dakota and flying to a good few more states. I was tracking down experts, raising support and money for the legal fees, uncovering old plots and pieces of corroborating evidences, demanding documents never sent to Jim by people taking advantage of his powerless incarcerated status. I wouldn't take no for an answer. I was quite "fresh off the boat", spoke only basic English, knew nothing of the law and the American judicial system. But—I could say with Dr. Martin Luther King—I had a dream. And I had no fear. Along the way, opposing forces tried stopping me through acts of intimidation, pressure, threats, bribes… you name it. In a few cases, things moved from 'unpleasant' to 'seriously dangerous'. Nothing stopped me from helping Jim, though. Nobody could convince me to give up.

I dedicated myself to a two-year investigation that led to new pieces of evidence thanks to Doctor Di Maio first, and the testimonies by even more pro bono experts. Terry Pechota, the attorney hired to reopen the case in habeas corpus, felt very confident. So did we. We presented the new evidence to Judge Rush during a hearing held in September 1995. We were positive that it would be just a matter of months. Judge Rush was going to review the new depositions that Terry Pechota and I had provided going to interview and question the people involved in the 1986 trial, from appointed defense attorney Lee A. Tappe to prosecutor Gary Conklin. Once he did this, he would see that the initial trial had been a joke and would free Jim. This Gary Conklin deposition, however, was curiously missing from the transcripts because the court reporter who should have transcribed it, had not submitted it in time. It was a crucial piece of evidence since Conklin's clearly demonstrated that the pathologist, Doctor Randall, had changed his opinion about the probable cause of death after conferring with the prosecutor: unacceptable by legal standards. Judge Rush accepted to have the hearing anyhow, counting on the court reporter to submit Conklin's deposition in a matter of days, but it never happened—not even when, after almost a year, the judge issued an order of arrest for her. The order was never executed. Cops went by her house and reported that she "had moved to an unknown destination." Incredibly, that was it for "serving the judge's order."

Totally frustrated by years of useless wait, James decided to give Judge Rush a green light to go ahead and form his judgment without Conklin's deposition. At that point, it was Judge Rush's turn to take his sweet time. Citing an urgent death penalty case he had on his plate that was taking up all his time and energy, the judge had us waiting several more years. And when his verdict finally came, it wasn't a favorable one. Long story short, we appealed to the Federal xz Supreme Court—our last shot; the very last possible step in this ten-year long marathon of legal proceedings. It took another inordinate amount of time for the Supreme Court to set a hearing in Armor, a town in Charles Mix County, South Dakota, close to Wagner, where the crime took place. But finally on the 18th of December 2003 our day came, and James walked out of that court a free man.

    The verdict didn't surprise us. The Supreme Court had already notified us that several irregularities in the original trial had been found. Terry, the prosecutor and the judge had then negotiated that Jim would plead guilty to a minor charge of assault to have his manslaughter sentence commuted to time served. Until it wasn't sanctioned, however, we were not going to party—not the two of us, not the whole family who couldn't wait to hug their Jimmy again, and honor him for his deeds as a warrior who never threw in the towel during this never-ending battle.

    We were all drunk without touching a drop of alcohol, that's what I remember the most of that day after we exited the Court. It had been chilly the night before, with a wicked blizzard blowing strong, but now the sun was shining and Jim couldn't keep his eyes open without shades on. We drove around in circles for a while, a procession of cars honking and full of excited, happy people. We stopped at a store for sodas. Jim wanted a Mountain Dew before heading to his brother Sam's house in Wagner, where many more people—those who couldn't make it to court—were waiting.

James celebrated by the family, on December 18th, 2003

James with the rest of the family waiting at Sam's house

Once again, for the millionth time in ten years, I was amazed about how cool Jim was, able to handle his emotions with grace, and yet generous even toward those who had abandoned him for the longest time. At some point, though, he dragged me in a corner and said: "I need a break. I cannot handle crowds. I know it's my family and I know they mean well and I love them, but I need some space. Let's take a ride."

He wanted to go by his mom's grave at the cemetery. The family had already been there with the court's decision, reading the verdict to Hazel so that she could party too.

Then, Jim wanted to go by the old place, the cabin where he was raised as a small child. It was nothing but a shack now, the windows broken and the grounds covered by weeds. "I'd fix it up", he said. "But four days are not enough."

Four days was the maximum time the court allowed him to spend in Charles Mix County. One of the three conditions of his seven-year

James on his mom's grave

probation term was, in fact, to live out of the county where he had been born and raised, and where his family lived. Why? His foes lived there as well and the court wanted to avoid potential problems. It was 2003, but in the court's estimate nothing had changed since 1986. The court seemed to fear that James' presence on the Yankton reservation could stir ancient resentments and be cause for new troubles.

The old cabin where James lived as a small child

No problem, decided James. "I'm probably not ready yet anyway. Some time in the Black Hills will restore my confidence. I'll be more fit to deal with people."

Wise words.

Eighteen years locked up don't get erased by a quick sponge bath. We drove up to Rapid City, which is just a few miles form the Black Hills, spent a few days at Terry's house, then a few more in a motel. I co-signed the rental agreement to a cute house in the foothills, far enough from crowds but still close enough to town. We had fun decorating it with thrift store furniture and handouts. The rental car we had driven from Wagner to Yankton was filled of pillows, throws, starblankets, and other gifts from the family. We went to the DMV to get his driver's license reissued, and then to buy a vehicle: a used, dark green Dodge 250 pickup, that Jim named "Sergio" after the Italian supporter who had donated the money to purchase it.

Life was starting all over again but there were simple things that Jim found himself unable to do. He couldn't eat in a restaurant, or go to a public laundry without getting paranoid that somebody was staring or following us. He was waking up in the middle of the night sure that he had heard somebody screaming or forcing their way through the entrance door. When, pretty soon, I had to leave and go back to Los Angeles, he got lonely and didn't know how to remedy it, forced to live 350 miles from his family. He had a few friends in Rapid and the close-by Pine Ridge reservation, but still had issues trusting people.

I spent the following year, 2004, back and forth between Los Angeles and Rapid City, and James came to visit anytime his parole officer would allow it.

Daniele and his grandma Zina, with James

This went on up until summer, when I packed my things and my dog, and drove the 1500 miles to South Dakota. I had found a job translating movies to be dubbed for the Italian market, something I could do on my laptop from anywhere, and Jim had started working as a sales representative for *Indian Country Today*, driving around all South Dakota reservations—something he had always enjoyed doing. It was a temporary solution since Jim had requested a transfer to California. I wasn't convinced that he could be happy so far removed from his family and people, but that was his choice back then. At the end of summer, I had to return to Los Angeles. When the board rejected Jim's request, it was a very bad blow.

If he couldn't move, then it was time to move on. Jim was just starting on the road to get back his place among his people. After spending some time by himself in the hills, in early 2005 he moved to Flandreau, on the Santee reservation, and started to work in the tribal construction company. Bad luck wasn't over, though. He had a wicked accident on a construction site, on August 30th. A hammer escaped the hands of a coworker and hit him in the face, right on his cheekbone, leaving him half paralyzed for a while and with permanent neurological damage. In October of the same year, James married Cyndi Allen, whom he had met when he arrived in Flandreau.

James and Cyndi on their wedding day

In January 2006, my sister Marina, still living in Italy, suffered a brain stroke. I left Los Angeles and the United States in a hurry, not knowing if I'd see her alive, and ended up spending most of the following four years in Italy, at her bedside. James and I communicated sporadically by letters and emails. My mind was totally occupied with my sister and his with the pain and worries following the accident but also, thanks goodness, with the new life that he was rebuilding for himself. After such a long separation, he had a lot of bonding still to do with his daughter and grandchildren. And his lifelong battle for the Black Hills called for his attention. No matter what the court had said, he still thought he could get them back.

We were finally able to get reunited only in July 2012. We had decided to meet in Rapid City and James drove all the way up. He was in great shape and mood, and we had a good time. He still had lots of trouble sleeping more than a few hours because of the pain in his face, but didn't want to spend his life swallowing a bunch of painkillers that "make me feel high and then fall so low like a drug addict." He was working in construction again but without pay. "I need to repay a debt, money spent on painkillers and treatment so, once again, I'm broke. Even this car I drove up with has been lent to me by a friend." Sergio, the green truck he loved so much, had been wrecked years earlier by a friend who took it for a ride. That's how James was. He'd never say no. If somebody needed his help, his truck or even his last dollar, he'd just give it to them. Friends, or even strangers. Big heart, little sense. He was wise only when it applied to others. Of the four virtues necessary to Lakota warriors, he had been loaded with extradoses of bravery, fortitude and generosity. But wisdom? He must have been going to take a leak at the moment they distributed this last virtue, and cultivating it without the seed had not brought remarkable results.

James in 2012

We stayed up all night before he had to go back to work, and share more stories about the seven years we hadn't seen each other. One of them was his reconciliation with Russell Means: a story that deserves to be told.

In the book *Agents of Repression*, author Ward Churchill told the tale of a gunfight that took place in the 1970s between James and other friends against AIM leader Russell Means and his own. In Churchill's version, James was a GOON—the term used for Indians paid by corrupted tribal governments to intimidate or kill political opponents—and the shootout was a carefully planned attempted execution against Means. This rendition of the story is so farcical as to be laughable if it weren't for the fact that it created major problems for James among AIM members and sympathizers. The most obvious clue indicating that Churchill made this up based on thin air is that James and Russell Means had both been supporters of Yankton AIM leader Greg Zephier, so clearly no major political disagreement existed.

But here's the never-before-published story of what actually happened, as Jim told me himself and others corroborated. Greg Zephier had invited Means to come to the Yankton reservation to help him with a few issues—among them was requesting Means' help to shield James when he was on the run from the law. They all got together at a party where a bad mix of alcohol and machismo set the shootout in motion. Everybody was already quite drunk when Means pointed at two guys present indicating he believed them to be FBI informers. The guys vocally denied this. Everyone else also said Means must be mistaken. They knew the two individuals, and there was no way they worked for the FBI. Unconvinced, Means reached for his gun indicating he'd shoot them down right there and then. James began yelling at Means that he was crazy and he better put his gun away. Grudgingly Means complied but the mood of the evening had radically changed. It wasn't long afterwards when more words were exchanged, guns were drawn, and Means and a friend of his ended up getting shot. By the time everyone had sobered up, they all would have liked to rewind the tape and erase what had happened from their lives. But it was too late.

The fact that the police investigating the shootout said that whoever had shot Means deserved a medal (such was their hatred against AIM) made James feel even more horrible about the whole thing. James always maintained that he never shot Russell Means, only tried to stop him from shooting two innocent guys. Others thought to join him in his efforts but went overboard and actually pulled the trigger. Everyone at the party was supposed to be on the same side. They were all fighting against the racism so prevalent in those days. And yet through their own mistakes, they had cast themselves as the helpers of the very racist system they were trying to fight. Going after each other's throat was the best favor they could have done to their enemies.

It was only after James was finally released from prison that he and Russell Means had a chance to be reunited, smoke the pipe together and renew their friendship. It was the summer of 2011, when Russell was visiting the Santee Reservation. He met Cyndi, James' wife and tribal vice-chairwoman. Hearing her last name, Russell asked her if she was related to Jim Weddell. When she said the he was her husband, Russell immediately asked her to summon him up, saying he'd like to see him.

Jim was nervous, not knowing what to expect, but as soon as he walked into the room, Russell said: "you didn't shoot me". "I know I didn't shoot you!" said James, "I've been repeating that all my life." They both started laughing about it and their reconciliation was sealed in the traditional way, smoking the pipe.

This was one of the highlights of James' last ten years of freedom, a story he'd never tire of recalling any time somebody asked about it.

In the instructions left for his service and funeral, James was adamant about how he wanted it to be done. He described every single detail. When it came to his ashes, he said: "Don't keep any. Let me go free. Spread them all over the Black Hills. Make sure to spread some at Yellow Thunder Camp so I will run around with Russell".

Russell Means and James, in 2011

Russell Means had passed from cancer one year before James, on October 22nd, 2012. I hope their spirits are having a good time in the Paha Sapa. I hope they run together up the trail to Harney Peak, roast t-bone steaks on the barbecues of Horse Thief campground, fish in the clear waters of Pactola and Sylvan Lakes. And if they still meet enemies on their path, I hope they count coup and kick their asses too.

One day, we'll be together again. *Doksa*, James, *doksa*.

About the author

Gloria Mattioni is the author of *Reckless-The Outrageous Lives of Nine Kick-Ass Women* (Seal Press, October 2005), and four other books previously published in Italy (among them, the novel *Con Altri Occhi*, and *La Tribù dei Mangiatori di Sogni*.) She lives in Los Angeles, contributing features to different media and producing documentaries. She is presently working at her new novel.

Made in the USA
San Bernardino, CA
10 September 2016